Family Matters
Hindsight 20/20

CO-AUTHORS

Rhonda Bankston,
Odessa Cegers, Derrie Davis,
Ruth Escarcega, Margo Williams,
Sharlita Monette Barrett
Jessica D.K. Romero

Family Matters
Hindsight 20/20

Book Prepared for Publication by:
TRU Statement Publications www.trustatementpublications.com

TRU Statement
PUBLICATIONS
www.trustatementpublications.com

Unless otherwise stated, all bible quotes have been taken from the King James Version (KJV)

Scripture taken from the New King James Version®. Copyright © 1982 by Thomas Nelson. Used by permission. All rights reserved.

THE HOLY BIBLE, NEW INTERNATIONAL VERSION®, NIV® Copyright © 1973, 1978, 1984, 2011 by Biblica, Inc.® Used by permission. All rights reserved worldwide.

The ESV® Bible (The Holy Bible, English Standard Version®). ESV® Text Edition: 2016.

First Printing: 2020
04042020

ISBN-13: 978-1-948085-37-3

CONTENTS

Letter from the Editor

hind·sight /ˈhīn(d)ˌsīt/

Hindsight is defined as an understanding of a situation or event only after it has happened or developed. One of life's biggest tragedies is to never stop and look back to discover, how or why life turned in the directions it did. For some, this is better said than done.

Sometimes, the only way we moved forward, past the pain, was by forgetting the past all together, but the infection of life will reappear if the area of pain and affliction was not healed. Because of the love of Jesus, we have the power to see life from a higher perspective; removing ourselves from the pit and seeing our life objectively from God's view.

Hindsight is 20/20. The moment we choose to look back and lean on God for understanding, we reach into the memory of our past and the mind of someone else's future. Once we receive the revelation of our trials, our testimonies and life lessons are keys to open doors which frees others from the wrong path taken and will lock the doors to ensure no one else will go down the path we once traveled.

We all have a life worth living, a life worth sharing, and a life worth saving. Our heavenly Father believed this, and Jesus Christ proved it.

To the Writers of this book, I thank you for your courage in surviving your past and being bold enough to share it. I pray many blessing to you for your obedience in the call of God and His will for your life.

To the Reader, I pray the testimonies shared in this book awaken the fighter, the warrior, and the lover of Jesus in you. Wherever you are, know that God is with you, He loves you, and will never forsake you.

Kaishia Slaughter
TRU Statement Publications

AKNOWLEDGEMENTS

To my sisters in Christ, by the blood, who have come together in this awesome book collaboration. Derrie Davis, Jessica Romero, Sharlita Barrett, Margo Williams, Rhonda Bankston, and Ruth Escarcega. I would like to thank you for your wonderful cooperation and participation during the planning process of it all.

The hindsight of all of this, is that I had no idea we would be writing a book together as one.

I would like to thank our wonderful Publisher Kaishia Slaughter, of TRU Statement Publications, for blessing us with the idea of a book collaboration to capture the stories of the speakers, for The Keys to the Kingdom's first Women's Conference, January 18, 2020. This is also a gift to honor the start of The Keys of the Kingdom Ministries International.

Thank you,

Odessa Cegers

PREFACE

Before you, is the layout of a book of stories, the chapters of lives women according to their point of view. The account of detailed and explicit stories of tragedies, challenges, teachable moments and triumphs. This book is a culmination of new courageous authors who decided to fight the fear and write anyway. With the strength and empowerment of God we overcame fear, shame, self-doubt, unbelief, and other inner challenges to complete this combined written work.

Fearlessly, we journeyed to our past with God's help to understand how Hindsight 20/20 protects us and conceals the things our past level of development could not properly interpret, that later would be revealed in the future. Certain knowledge & revelation gained to soon can be a detriment to one's development and capacity to handle certain truths and or revelations.

In retrospect we all have said to ourselves, "I wish I would have learned or understood the purpose of this along time of go." For some, denial has been a defense mechanism to maintain sanity of adverse circumstances. For others, God has his divine set time to remove the veil off the eyes of His people to enrich their lives and edify the body of Christ.

The preparation and writing process for many were scary and for some difficult due to the blunt story content in most of the writings. Conversely, how often do people reveal to the world their deepest darkest secrets? Leading to the opening of pandora's box.

Read this book and see the hindsight of your own personal life experiences. Understand that God is the one that can turn tragedies into triumphant stories of survival that leads on the path to destiny.

FAMILY MATTERS
Rhonda Bankston

Rhonda Bankston growing up in a Black middle class, Southern Baptist home in Pine Buff, Arkansas, where my mother was an educator and my father was a supervisor at the local paper mill. My mother was the church organist and the church clerk. My father was the choir director and a deacon. I was the church musician and my brothers sang in the choir. Growing up, I thought my mother was overprotective; she was the disciplinarian, and my father was easy going.

I was the girl in the middle of two boys, which always put me in the middle of everything. My older brother took care of me and I took care of my younger brother. My parents' marriage looked perfect. My brothers and I had the best clothing, went to the best schools, lived in the best neighborhood, had nice cars, and was involved in school, church, and community activities.

Three Black siblings on the National Honor Society, graduating with full academic scholarships. People thought that we were rich. My friends told me then, and now, "I wish Mr. and Mrs. Bankston were our parents."

My parents supported the school, church, and community fundraisers. They transported my friends, neighbors, and church members to work, church, school and doctors' appointments. They never asked anyone for gas money.

My maternal grandparents lived with us as well, which made life even greater! My grandfather was a letter carrier for the post office, and my grandmother was a housewife. My grandmother was the BEST cook in the world! We always had a housekeeper, who was our family friends.

Life was GREAT! It was not until I became an adult, that I realized that being married was not hard to do. The hard part was staying married. I guess it was hard for me to stay married, since I had two failed marriages.

I was married to two men that I had known all my life. My first husband grew up in my neighborhood. He was in my graduating high school class. He was someone that I saw every day in the neighborhood. My house was the hang out. Every day after school most of the neighborhood kids would come to our house. We had a basketball goal on the driveway, a pool table in the garage, a pinball machine in the playroom, and we could play kickball, softball, or football in the front yard.

I remember my first husband's father being a Vietnam era veteran, and his mother being a housewife. In the neighborhood, we had always heard "Mr. Johnson" was crazy, because he had been to war. The people said that he did not come back the same. They said he had a metal plate in his head. His mother always seemed afraid to talk. She was quiet but always smiling.

After marrying her son, and after he exited the Army, I realized why our marriage did not work. My first marriage ended in domestic violence. I had never known him to be a fighter, but I guess I really did not know him. I listened to his military stories over and over again; I listened to all of the countries that he had been to, not knowing that I would be a Registered Nurse working at a local VA medical center and working with homeless veterans 30 years later.

I did not realize he had anger problems along with drinking problems. One night, he had been out in a local club drinking with another childhood friend, who had happened to be my friend and my next-door neighbor when we were growing up. He came home late one hot Saturday night in July, beating on the front door yelling and demanding that I let him in the house.

In fear of my safety, because I had never experienced anything like this before, I was afraid to let him in the house. He was yelling so loudly that the noise awakened the neighbors. Can you imagine how shocked and embarrassed I was? I could not believe it! When I opened the door, he punched me in the face and knocked me to the living room floor. I struggled kicking and punching him off me. I grabbed everything I could put my hands on in an attempt to get away from him.

Because he was so drunk, he finally got tired and passed out on the living room floor. I dragged myself to the bedroom and cried myself to sleep. In the middle of the night, he hit me again, demanding that I "make love" to him. The nerve of him! I was afraid not to, so, I did! It was disgusting! I felt violated! It felt like a nightmare. It was almost time for me to get up to take a shower to prepare for church. I could not believe what was happening to me.

As I was showering, I saw the bruises, scratches, and dried blood on my arms, neck, legs. I could not stop crying. When I got out of the shower, he was standing at the door telling me he was sorry. All I could think in my head was, "Yes! You are sorry!"

It was going to be 105 degrees that Sunday. As I stood in my closet looking for a dress to cover up the bruises and scratches I thought, "What will people think at the church when they see me? What will they say?" All I could think was, "I am not going to stay in this! I am leaving today!"

I got ready for church. I put on a long maxi dress with a high collar and long sleeves. I know I must have really looked crazy. As hot as it was, with ALL these clothes on. I drove to church, which was around the corner from my house. I walked into church, walked to the piano, smiling as if nothing happened. I am an ACTOR! I had been in church, school and community productions. I knew I could play this off and nobody would ever know. Not the church girl who had the GREAT life. DOMESTIC VIOLENCE! RHONDA BANKSTON? NO! NEVER!

I made it through the entire service. I was playing the piano. My dad was directing the choir. My mother was playing the organ. My brothers were in the choir stand. I felt that they knew something was wrong.

Well, "MY HUSBAND" walked into church, which he never does. He was not the church boy. He did not grow up in church and never went to church. He did not want me to go to church either! This guy acted like nothing happened. He was a better actor than I was. After church service was over, he was speaking to everyone like everything was wonderful! I was afraid to speak.

After church, I went to my parents' house. My entire family knew that something was wrong. I was sitting and thinking about a plan to come back to live at my parents' house. I did not want to make a scene. I was not going to spend another night with him. My mother offered me dinner and asked me did my husband want to eat dinner as well.

By the time my mother asked me about him, he rang the doorbell. He had the nerve to ask me did I want to go to lunch. I sat down at the table, but I could not eat. I felt my stomach in knots. I told my mother that I was going with my husband. My mother had a look on her face as if she feared for me. We left and went home.

One particular day, my younger brother, who was a freshman in college in Fayetteville, AR, and I were going to the mall so he could get school supplies. When my younger brother, my protector, came to my house for a ride to the mall, I had pulled off my church jacket to put on something casual to go shopping. My brother saw the bruises and scratches. He asked me, "What the hell happened to you?"

I said, "Nothing." By this time, my husband told my brother that it was time for him to go home. At that point I feared for my brother's safety. My husband called his father who was known to always carry a gun. His father was at my front door yelling, "Nobody leaves my son! Little boy you need to go home before I bust a cap in your ass!"

I froze in my tracks and demanded that my brother go home. My brother told me he was not leaving me. He said, "He will never put his hands on you again!"

My little brother, my protector, growing up to be a man, took me to my parents' house. My older brother met us walking down the street. I was crying uncontrollably. When I got home, my parents and grandparents told me that I did not have to stay with him in a domestic violence relationship. They all told me that he will always beat me if I stayed with him. I stayed at my parents' home and never went back.

Now I know that I was blessed and I still am. I know that my parents had issues like anybody else, but they never let us know. If my parents had a disagreement, they discussed it in their bedroom. They always made us feel loved and important. I was a daddy's girl. I got everything that I wanted.

Family is the first line of defense. Through my embarrassment and fear, my family helped me through this crisis. I felt that I had done something wrong to cause this fight, this abuse, this anger, this rage. This was not love. What I learned was, if I had stayed with this man who said that he loved me, it would have now been over thirty years of fighting, anger, rage, hurt, or even death. I could have gone for years hearing, "I am sorry."

I encourage everyone who is contemplating marriage, date and get to know the immediate family, discuss childhood issues, domestic violence, mental illness, physical illness, physical abuse, sexual abuse, psychological abuse, long term and short term goals, posttraumatic stress syndrome, stressors, likes and dislikes, death and life.

MEET THE WRITER

Rhonda Bankston

HINDSIGHT LOVE
Odessa Cegers

INNER WEALTH
Excerpt from Poetry for the Soul
Written by Odessa Cegers

Inner Wealth

The diamond in the rough, a hidden jewel to discover.

No longer overlooked, it's time to recover.

Hidden in obscure and rare situations

You're discovered by those with wise observation.

Overlooked by the common ones, you see

A new platform very soon to be.

Your shine will come forth, it's a matter of time

Embodying great treasures, resources of its kind.

Your priceless worth, some can see from the start

Your bold new shine sets you apart.

Treasure chest inside you unfold

Endless possibilities with far reaches untold.

<u>Affirmations for Inner Wealth</u>

1. Inner wealth flows into my life daily.

2. I tap into endless possibilities of inner peace.

3. I activate inner strength and healthy thinking

4. New opportunities of success await me daily

5. My life is filled with increasing numbers of abundance in every area of my life.

<u>Introduction</u>

There are many things people pride themselves on in life. Some money, career, status, power, etc. Mine, was on the power of seduction. The irony in all of this is I was unaware of this unknown subtle behavior. The graphic memories of my childhood trauma molded and shaped my life into a glob of confusion on the inside, while carefully crafted an appealing false sense of self on the outside. To share my story with you, the reader, is one of the most challenging steps I have ever taken in my life. There will be a full book that will emerge from this chapter book in this collaboration piece. Writing a full book of my life has to be written in volumes.

It was, and still is, a fight to reveal the skeleton's in my closet or open pandoras box. One goal is to unveil and allow myself to be naked and transparent with faith that my story will set many captives free. This book collaboration will only address details that deal with how Satan attempted to destroy me using sex to derail me from reaching my purpose and destiny.

I write for the little girl inside of me that could not speak for herself. The little girl inside that never felt protected, heard, supported, or validated. I speak to little Odessa, as the Adult, strong protective one, and I tell you how strong brave and smart you are. I use the keys to the Kingdom, and I unlock the prison cell of the past. I release you from the bondage that shut you down from operating in ministry for over 20 years. This New Year of 2020, I am here to remind you, despite all your adversities you were supportive to your family, friends, community, even to your enemies.

Through your homelessness, isolation, betrayal, rejection, poverty, nakedness, sufferings, etc. God has pulled you out of the furnace of affliction to use for His will and His Glory. Amen!

This Hindsight 20/20 chapter deals with behaviors that ruled my life for over 40 years. How my soul was fragmented. How I controlled the start and stopping of romantic encounters. I will provide details about my awakening to God, the damages I had done to myself and others. I am going to take you on a journey in raw explicit details that will stir your emotions.

My second goal with sharing my story is to help you, the reader, reexamine your own past and the past of others around you, in order to heal and start the process of deliverance, healing, and wholeness.

My last Goal is that my story will help you understand the power of forgiving others in order to reach great heights of purpose and destiny. So, brace yourself and take a ride with me on the rocky road in the time machine of my life.

For years I lived a life driven by impulses that stemmed deep from inside my wounded soul. Like a siren seeking her next prey to fill the emptiness, I too searched for validation and affirmation in the bedroom, with the illusion of finding someone that would approve of me in my broken and empty state. My story will vividly show you how strongholds come in many layers.

Soul Fragmentation Process: The Early Years

It was a summer day in Chicago, as I a sat in the back seat of my mother's boyfriend's car. We were planning to go to Rainbow Beach for a cookout. My mother was upstairs getting some items that she left in the house. Her boyfriend came to the back seat and sat next to me. I don't remember him saying very much. Except for, "Do you like?" while he took his fingers and rubbed the imprint of my blue jean shorts.

I sat there confused and didn't respond to the question. He quickly moved back to the front of the car as my mother returned to the car. It never crossed my mind to tell my mother what happened. There was never a conversation to prepare me for the possibility of being violated by a pedophile. We went to the beach and I forgot about the altercation altogether. I suppressed the incident in my mind to forget it ever happened.

Later on, my family moved; when I was 7 years old the molestation happened again. Except this time, it escalated to something worse. I remember being sleep and awakened to my mother boyfriend rubbing my vagina area. I remember abruptly waking up and him quickly removing his hand from my panties. This happened several times and stopped for about 2 years. Still I did not share this with anyone.

The last altercation was the age of nine years old. Even though it was a stretch of time, the molestation was going from one level to another. The encounter I remember was one evening after dinner. I remembered being pulled into a closet and I was made to touch his penis while he still had his pants on. I squeezed his penis as hard as possible and kicked him. He screamed! I quickly left the closet. My mother came in the room and asked what was going on! I said nothing and went silent. Her boyfriend lied on me and said that I grabbed his private area.

With anger I shouted loudly, "No Momma, it was him. He pulled me in the closet and made me touch him. That's Why I kicked him!"

My mother looked at me in shock! She stood there stuck! I told her, "Mom, he has been touching me for years in the car and while I was sleeping at night."

My mother told me to quiet down and not to share this with my brothers and uncle, because they would kill him. I said to mom, "Are you going to make him leave?"

My mother was conflicted, and she turned and walked away. I loved my mother and obeyed her wishes not to share this issue with anyone. For years I kept the incidents a secret.

Indecent Exposure

At 12 years old I spent an overnight at a friend's house. It seemed like a good idea to get away from all the fighting and arguing going on at my house. Little did I know, there was a 21-year-old guy that was living with my friend's family. My friend had a sofa couch and we were getting ready to go to bed. My friend went to the bathroom to get ready for the night. The guy came and laid down next to me. He didn't say anything but started taking off my clothes and told me he was going to make me feel good.

I told him to stop, and I began trying to push him off me. His strength overpowered me, and he penetrated me. I cried silently while he thrust himself into me. After about 5 minutes, my friend flushed the toilet. He quickly got off of me and went into the kitchen. I checked my private area and blood was on my finger. After seeing the blood, I laid on the sofa bed hysterically crying with my head in the pillow. I felt broken, worthless, and destroyed. My friend asked me what's wrong, what's wrong, why are you crying.

I told her what happened, and she didn't look surprised at all. "Did he do this to you too?"

She didn't say anything. I thought to myself, "This is not new to you at all."

I started wondering if I was set up by her. The next day I went home and refused to go outside for 2 weeks straight, because this same friend spread rumors about me and put fake blood in the hallway. She fabricated lies about me in the neighborhood.

I did not share this with my mother or anyone else, because I felt that no one would do anything about it. Once again, I felt betrayed and unprotected.

Hindsight Scripture

Walk with the wise and become wise,

for a companion of fools suffers harm.

Proverbs 13:20

The seed of fear, rejection, and abuse was sown at very early stages of my life, and as a result, my soul was fragmented, and wounds developed. At 14 I determined that no one would touch me without my consent. Growing up in Chicago, I witnessed constant violence and learned how to fight to protect myself. I became hardened and calloused by the experiences.

My first conscious sexual encounter was with a boy who was 16 years of age. He was my first sexual consented experience. I felt strong and in control, because I had the choice to choose. The experience was different, and I enjoyed it. For the next 2 years my sexual encounters were infrequent.

Hidden in Plain Sight

At the age of 16, I start back hanging out with this same girl that betrayed me. She was stabbed by her mother's boyfriend and needed somewhere to live; the man who stabbed her was not reported, nor made to leave. I had flashbacks of what happened to me and nothing was done to protect me. So, I decided to protect her by helping her. I begged my mother to take in my friend, since her home life was too dangerous. My mother reluctantly took her in. One day we were in the room listening to music and she said I have something for us to watch and I said, "Ok cool."

I looked up and noticed that it was a porn on the screen. I was shocked and said girl you are crazy. It was a scene of 2 girls making out with each other. I asked her why you are watching this and not a man and a woman. She paused it and said she could turn it off if it was bothering me. Succumbing to the peer pressure, I agreed to watch it with her out of curiosity, but I felt disgusted as I watched this flic with her.

I told her I seen enough I'm straight and ended the movie. It was silence, and she asked me had I ever had an experience with a girl. I told her no and expressed how much I love sex with guys only. She asked me if I would like to try it one day. I said, "No!"

Right away I knew that she had experienced being with a girl. I asked her to confirm what I already knew, and she told me that she experienced being with girls several times. My feet and hands grew cold and I shook my head. She then boldly asked me would I like to try it for myself. I told her, "Girl, I literally have cold feet right now and I am scared to try it."

I thought to myself how much I was starting to hate men after all the terrible things that happened to me. Subconsciously, the only thing that motivated me to try out the experience was that I had the power of choice. She convinced me that I didn't have to do anything and to lay back and promised that I would enjoy the experience. So, allowed it, and I enjoyed it, but felt shame and remorse afterwards. That one-time encounter led to several experiences. We both eventually decided to stop and move on; in my life like nothing ever happened. This was a new layer of sexual experience that shattered my soul and opened me up to bondage.

One month later, she started leaving early and would come back late in the evening, but always had a pocket full of money. One day she came to the house with new clothes. I asked her, "Where did you get the clothes?"

"I was working with this man and he paid me," she said. She pulled out $40 dollars and said let's go get something to eat.

I was relieved, because I was so hungry due to my family constantly running out of food toward the end of the month. After we ordered the food, she said to me, "You know you can come work for him daily and you get paid the same day?"

I said, "Yes girl, please tell me how I can get hired."

So, she took me to meet this man and he asked me why should he hire me? I shared that I cleaned houses and I worked summer jobs as a camp counselor. He asked me, "Why do you feel the need to work, don't your family take care of you?"

I told him that I would use the money to help care for my family. In addition, I needed school clothes, because September was around the corner.

He nodded his head and said, "I see," while he undressed me with his eyes. I felt uncomfortable but ignored what I saw and worked for him that day with my friend. I was so happy to make the money.

Weeks later, the friend came to the house with bags of new clothes. I said, "Girl, where did you get all those clothes?"

She said, "You know, working."

I looked at her in disbelief and said, "Now you know that money is not enough to get that many outfits. Tell me the truth!"

She looked off in disgust and I looked at her and I shouted, "Tell me!"

She said it came from our boss, but I asked her why he would just buy her school clothes and she is not his child. She said she would tell me, but I could not tell anyone! I promised her I would not to share the information.

She said that he asked to see her breasts and gave her $600 dollars.

$600 dollars!" I said, "And he didn't want anything else, no sex?"

She said no sex. She told me he asked about me and if I needed anything extra. I looked at her with disgust. "If you need clothes all you have to do is who some tits. It's not like you having sex with him!"

She set up the meeting, and he asked me if he could help me with something. I said clothes and shoes for school. He asked me "Can I see your breast?"

I stood their nervous and grossed out. He pulled the money out and laid it out on the table. "How much is that I asked?"

He said, "$600 dollars. All you have to do is raise your shirt up and let me see."

So, I raised my shirt up and he looked for a few minutes, gave me the money and I left.

When I walked home, I felt like everyone I passed knew what I had done. I felt ashamed, with a deep feeling of worthlessness. I started feeling like I hated men altogether, starting with my father who rejected me when I was 11 years old. I tried calling my father and he hung the phone up on me.

The next encounter with the man and the money, was he offered me more money if I let him touch my nipple. He offered me more money, so I agreed. Each encounter increased and I eventually had full fledge sex with him. I was so grossed out with sleeping with a man that was old enough to be my grandfather.

With each sexual encounter I got paid more money, but my soul was being destroyed. I learned to detach myself from the experience in order to take care of myself and feed my family.

Later I move with a family member to escape physical and emotional abuse I was undergoing with one of my eldest brothers at home. Due to my mother's mental health challenges and her inability to address issues, she did not remove my brother from our home, so I often moved in and out, back and forth from home for several years.

While living with the family who was connected to us by way of marriage, the brother of the distant relative lived in the home with us. One day I was left alone with the person and he started making sexual advances at me. I tried to resist the encounter, but the individual kept pressuring me to have sex with him. So, I told him, "Do what you want and get it over with."

I laid there quiet, motionless, and I blacked out with the experience. I remember telling myself that I was good for nothing but someone's sex object and accepted what I believed was my fate in life.

Boundaries Destroyed

This encounter led me to becoming a call girl as my own little side hustle while in high school. I would meet men who I would see or date exclusively for exchange for sex and money. Eventually, I became good at concealing that part of my life and became highly skilled sexually by the age of 18 years old.

I prided myself on my physical appearance and my ability to make men fall in love with me. I fell in love with developing the art of seduction. Understanding the seduction was a process; for some men it was slow and some fast. Seducing men became a sport especially when no sex was involved. Despite those traits, I always treated the men with kindness, listened to them when they shared their hurts, fears, disappointments, marital problems, and dreams. I genuinely took interest in who they were, even their potential.

There were men that wanted to leave their wives and be with me. Doctors, Executives, Businessmen, and men from all walks of life. However, I kindly turned them down and sent them home to work out their differences; teaching them how to please their wife or significant other, who didn't know how to ask for what they wanted in the bedroom. After listening to them I had sex with them and took their money.

I found it hard to stop because the money was used to help provide for myself and feed my family. The boundary I did set was that my friends' boyfriends were not an option and they were off limits. I had situations that my friends guy tried to come on to me and I shut it down.

My mother had no idea what I was doing. I was allowed too much freedom, because I played a strong supportive role to my mother. There was a role reversal due to my mother's challenges with mental health. I loved my mother, in spite of all the things that happened to me and remained loyal.

Going Forward in Time

At 18 years old, I got pregnant with my first child. I was introduced to my eldest son dad, and got pregnant the first sexual encounter, instantly. The father did not believe that he could get someone pregnant, because his relationship before me was a duration of 5 years, and she did not get pregnant. This new additional rejection experience reminded me of what I went through with my father. I felt devastated and the previous wounds of my own father were deepened as a result.

After getting pregnant with my first born, I did not want to raise my son in Chicago. My eldest brother died a tragic death in 1991 and I vowed if I ever had children, I would do my best to protect them. The goal was to place them in environments where crime and drugs were less or reduced.

At the age of 18 years old, 4 months pregnant, I quit my job and moved to Minneapolis where my sister lived; however, the family did not know where my sister was due to extenuating circumstances she was facing. I called and searched, and eventually found my sister in a neighboring city or what is called twin city of Saint Paul Minnesota.

I was relieved to be away from Chicago for various reasons. One, Minnesota was a safe place to raise a family, with jobs and various opportunities to move forward. In addition, my life changed drastically after getting pregnant and it slowed me down from the promiscuous behavior.

Since the age of 17, I remember having an awareness of the presence of God. I was not raised in church, but anytime my mother was invited, I remember being the only one that was gamed to go. I used to pray to God to help me stop fornicating and committing adultery.

During the nine months I spent alone while pregnant, I started praying to God about the future of my son. I wanted to start pleasing God and stop sleeping around. So, I started thinking, if I gain weight, I could ward off men from talking to me. I didn't trust myself and started eating. I later begin to use food as a defense mechanism. Which later turned into a stronghold that I am still confronting until this day.

How Los Angeles Saved My Life

In 1997, I met a young lady with 2 children while standing at the bus stop in Minneapolis. She was a victim of domestic violence. I noticed she had a broken leg and her family was shivering cold. I asked her if she was okay and what happened to her leg.

She stated she was fleeing a domestic violence situation and was homeless, because she refused to go back. Immediately without question, I offered the family a place to stay. She told me she was not from Minnesota and wanted to get back home with her family. I assured her that I would help get her back.

The family stayed with me for 2 months, and I never thought to ask her where she was from. I moved to another apartment and offered the family to come and stay with me. We moved in Mid-December and she expressed to me she was ready to go back home. I finally asked her where she was from. She smiled and said Los Angeles.

I shouted, "You're from LA? I love LA and always imagined visiting out there."

Without hesitation, I asked her how soon did you want to go back home? She said New Year's Day she wanted to travel. So, I called a travel agent and booked the flight.

She expressed that she was afraid to fly and wanted to take the Greyhound Bus. I laughed and said, "You must be insane to take a bus from here, all the way to Los Angeles." Reluctantly, I agreed to take the long trip to LA, with kids on the Greyhound bus.

New Year's Eve we started packing to leave for the trip. I was so excited that I was leaving the torturing below zero weather of Minnesota. While planning for the trip I was drinking champagne, high from smoking and packing the night before. I heard an audible voice say to me, *"If you don't turn to the Lord your God you shall surely die."*

I looked around the room to see where the voice came from. I shook it off and thought I was high or maybe the marijuana was laced without my knowledge. I continued to pack, and I heard the voice again; this time it said, *"Go get your ex-husband's bible and turn to the book of Deuteronomy."*

I looked around the room and then I recognized that it was God's voice I was hearing. I got the bible and He said, "Turn to the 28th chapter."

The bible was a study bible that had titles for various sections. The Lord said read the part about the curses not the blessings. I read about the curses, got scared, and dismissed it after I read it. I went to bed and suppressed the experience in the back of my mind. The next morning, we boarded the Greyhound bus and set out on the long exciting journey to Los Angeles.

On the way there I kept experiencing God's presence in various states; like in Colorado, tears began to roll down my face as I pierced into the mountains and the stars in the night. It was something very special about the mountains. We finally arrived in downtown Los Angeles.

I saw the people sleeping in tents homeless, prostitutes, drug attics, etc. I started crying on the bus, my friend kept asking me what's wrong with you? I told her I don't know! However, deep down inside I knew God was dealing with me for some reason. I told my friend that I would one day help the homeless and open shelters and feed them. She looked at me and said, "Girl you are crazy."

I looked at her and shrugged my shoulders, but little did I know, I discovered my purpose. I understood it was meant for me to help her, because she was the connection to coming to CA.

Immediately, I felt that God was telling me to relocate to Los Angeles. To leave everything and don't look back. It was a tough decision, because I had just moved to a beautiful townhome in a Minneapolis Suburb. However, the beautiful palm trees and the 75-degree weather in the month of January was pulling me.

My friend told me she was not going back with me to Minneapolis and do whatever I wanted to do with our stuff. So, I went back home to sell all my furniture. But one day, I went out with friends and I was in a terrible accident. The vehicle, a family friend was driving, skidded on black ice and the truck flipped 3 times. No one was hurt and I only had a scratch on my knee. I heard a voice say to me on the ride back home, *"Didn't I tell you not to leave LA and to give up everything and don't look back?"*

I started crying and my friends said what's wrong. I told them that I know why we had the accident. I was not supposed to leave Los Angeles. They looked at me and said I was crazy. Two weeks later, I sold everything and moved to Los Angeles with the family I met.

However, it did not work out, because the family living conditions were not up to par.

I met a Pastor through a mutual person. He said, "Sister, can I pray for you?" I agreed to let him pray and immediately, he said "I see God snatching you out of the devil's hands. Sister, if you don't turn to the Lord, your God, you shall surely die!"

I shouted, "Oh my God! God told me this before coming to LA!"

I eventually found a place in San Fernando Valley, where the rent was more affordable. The enemy started planting seeds in my mind about starting my very own brothel, and where I could find clients in the West and North Hollywood area who had money. I started meeting pretty girls that were in abusive relationships, broke, homeless, and hated men. I would ask them if their guy friends were paying their bills or if they were giving them money for spending the night with them. In all cases the girls said, "No!"

I would laugh them to shame and say to them, "As pretty as you are, why are you broke!" They were scared to ask the guys for money and wait for them to offer gifts or money. Many times, the girls were the ones spending money on the guys. I started sharing secrets with them on how to get money out of guys; how to run game on men. They would follow my advice and would report to me that they were getting money.

Later I asked the girls if I was able to set them up with a man that would pay them to go on a date $500 dollars, would they do it? They were excited agreed to be part of the plan to get paid. I begin making plans to set up transactions. Little did I know, God had a greater plan.

I met a man on the bus who was clearly and older guy, but handsome and well dressed. He started talking to me and asked for my phone number. The whole time while conversing with him, I was planning to see how I can get some money out of him. He eventually started calling me and it was always when I was getting ready to go out to a club in Hollywood.

One day, he asked me if he could pray for me before I went to the club. I took a long pause and told the man that I did not feel comfortable praying before going to the club. He explained that the prayer was for my protection. So, I agreed and let him pray for me.

After getting off the phone my friend asked me who was that. I told her it was the guy I met, and he wanted to pray for me. I told her, if he ever calls back, lie; tell him I was away.

One day I answered the phone and he started talking about God. I told the man that I love God and all, but I was not ready to change. He ignored me and invited me to the church he was attending at the time. I declined and hung up the phone. I attempted to continue planning a service and setting up transactions to transform women into call girls, but every attempt began to unravel at the seams. God blocked all attempts.

The Awakening Moment

One night I stood in the kitchen and said to God, "If you are real, take me to a church where there is Power." So, I called the evangelist guy and told him I was finally ready to go to church. I went after Christmas, going into the new year. My life changed dramatically.

In 2000 the Lord told me that he wanted me to go into full time ministry and that he wanted to transform my life. I had a hard time believing it and the enemy used carnal believers to inflict church hurt for reasons I did not understand. Unfortunately, I did not understand that the church people can be just as cruel as people in the world.

In addition, I needed lots of deliverance. The enemy caused my life to go in circles in the spiritual desert of life for 20 years.

Hindsight:

Just because someone goes to church does not mean their character has been refined. Often times, many churches are filled with immature carnal Christians that are still drinking milk; versus being mature and eating the meat of the word of God. They were weak links easily influenced and used by the enemy. It's unfortunate that the enemy has blinded all of us from seeing our sinful ways. Pride has a way of making you think you are okay, when you are not.

1 Corinthians 3:1

And I, brethren, could not speak to you as to spiritual people but as to carnal, as to babes in Christ.

Hindsight Theory

The voids of not having a relationship with my father and the beginning interactions with men in relation to molestation, rape, and simply selling my body to survive had adverse effects. The effects led to prostitution, 2 broken marriages, 3 children with different fathers, bi-sexual encounters, porn, and other related addictions. Some of the areas I continued to struggle with, even after the attempt to surrender my life over to God.

Hindsight

➤ I lacked the necessary knowledge and understanding and addressing generational curses.

1 Corinthians 6:16

What? Know ye not that he who is joined to a harlot is one body with her? "For two," saith He, "shall be one flesh."

➤ You also sleep with every person that the one you had sex with had as well.

Titus 3:5

Not by works of righteousness which we have done, but according to His mercy He saved us, through the washing of regeneration and renewing of the Holy Spirit

➤ Just because we say the sinners pray and attend church services, does not mean that all the residue and garbage of the past, in the soulish realm, are rectified. In the spirit I am free, but the flesh has to die to self. It's important to go through discipleship, deliverance and healing.

Generational curses - Numbers 14:18

The LORD longsuffering, and of great mercy, forgiving iniquity and transgression, and by no means clearing, visiting the iniquity of the fathers upon the children unto the third and fourth generation.

The Walk of Shame

I had failed ministry attempts in 2012 after becoming a licensed minister, where I quickly gave up the license. I got pregnant with my last child and felt devastated and ashamed; I hated myself for my failures. I was confused as to how I could love God but was still so trapped deep in sin. The Lord revealed to me that I needed deliverance from all the transferred spirits, from generational curses, sin, rejection, trauma, bitterness, resentment, and the list goes on.

The soul ties were numerous, because spirits transfer through sex, drugs, and porn addiction; therefore, many open spiritual wounds flooded my life. I developed many strongholds, chains, yokes, and had no knowledge as to how to overcome the spiritual bondage.

After many failed attempts to find churches that fully understood deliverance, taught on the subject, or even acknowledged believers needed it, I continued to go through life broken, defeated, and powerless. I begin to ask the Lord to reveal to me the mysteries of my life. He revealed to me that many demons don't travel alone, and they have certain groupings or familiar spirits.

Matthew 12:43-45

When an unclean spirit comes out of a man, it passes through arid places seeking rest and does not find it. Then it says, 'I will return to the house I left.' 25On its return, it finds the house swept clean and put in order. 26Then it goes and brings seven other spirits more wicked than itself, and they go in and dwell there. And the final plight of that man is worse than the first."

Protect and maintain your deliverance by keeping your house clean This is why many Ministers fail due to the lack of knowledge.

30

I begin to repent, pray, and eventually started fasting to address and confront the strongholds over my life. I often had to stay on one prayer point to see the beginning of a breakthrough. I was beginning to learn how to fight; to pick up my sword and learn to pray so my life would change dramatically.

In addition, I learned how to ask for the help of the Holy Spirit; to help me pray on a consistent basis. My biggest hindsight awakening was that I had no idea how to fight. Fight and stand using the Word of God. I learned how the full of Army of God is a lifestyle.

If these areas are out of bounds or the person is not working to develop them, you are in trouble and will live a life of defeat.

- ❖ **Helmet**: Salvation is a lifestyle:
- ❖ **Shoes**: Peace is a lifestyle
- ❖ **Girdle**: Truth is a lifestyle
- ❖ **Shield**: Faith is a lifestyle
- ❖ **Sword**: Word of God
- ❖ **Breast Plate**: Righteousness is a lifestyle

Another Hindsight Strategy is I had prayer points such as:

➢ I prayed to God to change my story to give Him the Glory.

➢ Lord destroy every generational curse operating in my family by fire.

➢ Lord show me how to use your Word to overcome life challenges.

My prayer is that my story will encourage the body of Christ to deal with the hidden sins of flesh, the lust the eyes, the lust of the flesh, and the pride of life.

I am still in the process of learning how to pray the Word over my life, to apply the scripture strategically and intentionally to specific situations.

Odessa Cegers

Odessa Cegers is the Pastor of Keys of the Kingdom Ministries International in Orange County, California. She is a published author of the book, *Poetry for the Soul: Discovering Your Inner Potential.*

Odessa's background is in public speaking, addictions counseling, entrepreneurship, case management, life skills training, homeless prevention.

Odessa is available for book discussions, speaking engagements, workshops, and appearances.

Contact: ktkministries@gmail.com

ODESSA CEGERS

THE RIDE OF MY LIFE
Sharlita Monette Barrett

The Innocence of a Child

As a little girl, before life happened, before my parents' divorce, before my divorce, and before many other trials in life, I had a dream of one day meeting my Prince Charming, my Knight in shining armor; getting married and galloping out into the sunset as we lived happily ever after. How many of us still have this dream?

We all have a little girl inside of us who was once full of confidence, dreams, hope, boldness, and limitless possibilities, but somewhere along the journey of life, broken hearts developed, unforgiveness, bitterness, broken dreams, insecurities, settling for less than our worth, and even some walls from fear of trusting again. If you will allow me, I would like to invite you to travel with me on a journey of my life in a condensed version of the last 43 years; first as the little girl full of vision and endless possibilities, then to the 33 year old woman who lost herself in pain, and finally to the new best version of me I'm becoming at 43 years old, full of vision, destiny, and hope again!

Life Full Circle

When I was born, I lived in Pomona, CA, but was born in Fontana, CA, at Kaiser Hospital. My mom and dad were married, and I had an older sister who was six years older than me at that time. Our family was non-practicing Catholics; however, we always knew the Lord's prayer and believed in Jesus, we just didn't know Him or have a relationship with Him. My childhood wasn't very stable, but I didn't realize that until about nine years of age when seeing my mom and dad divorce.

We moved around a lot from Inland Empire, CA, to Texas, to Compton, CA, to South Gate, CA, then to Long Beach, CA. Growing up, I had a passion for the arts, music, dancing, singing, acting, gymnastics, cheer, tap, ballet, jazz, track, softball, and basketball. With so much creativity and no guidance, I was open to many childhood and teenage traumas and attacks like child molestation, rape, gangs, drugs, hustling, promiscuity, etc.

Having a loving father who was an alcoholic, was equivalent to having a father who was never really there. In that, I was looking for love in all the wrong places. I went through life looking for the acceptance and affirmation I never received from my dad. The Lord created the family unit as a type and shadow of what the Body of Christ is and the Family in God. Our earthly father is to be the representation of our heavenly Father, but when your earthly father doesn't know the Lord Jesus and is broken, how can he know how to love a daughter?

He Kept My Mind

At seventeen years of age, in 1993, I gave my life to Christ, but was never discipled. As the years progressed and after many lessons, on what I thought was love and lessons on life, I encountered love, Himself, at 28 years old; my life was radically saved at that time in 2004. I had an encounter with Jesus in my home in Long Beach, CA, and I never looked back. He literally moved me from Long Beach, CA (*My Egypt*), back to the Inland Empire, the very land I was born in. Full circle, God brought me right back to the land of my inheritance.

I was a single mom of three and had my son in my womb during my exodus out of Egypt. The Lord taught me so much during that time of my life. He quickly discipled me, threw me into seminary, and pushed me into ministry. Being a single woman on fire for God, with children and desiring to be married, a few years later I met someone who I "thought" was a man of God and portrayed to be a man of God at the time. I fell in love and married him, even after I saw all the red flags in our relationship prior to marriage.

A few months into the marriage I began to see another side of him that I wasn't ready for. The Lord began to reveal to me this was not His perfect will, but His permissible will. I was so desperate and broken at what I thought was love was actually a familiar spirit on assignment to destroy me and my children's prophetic destiny. God had to reveal to me there was still something rising up in me that I needed to crucify; it was the lust of the flesh.

How many times as women, do we think we can change someone for the better and/or even lead a man to Christ? Somewhere in the process of this marriage shame, fear, guilt, condemnation, confusion, and loss of purpose began to take over me and my children. There was a lot of verbal and emotional abuse that was leading to physical abuse, if I would have continued in the relationship. Deep rooted rejection and abandonment began to rise up in me even as I prayed, fasted, counseled, and believed God to restore my marriage; but instead, God exposed the adultery and sin he was in and removed him.

I even took him back to my own demise, justifying that it was better to be reconciled, but again God removed him and gave me a firm word of warning, *if I took him back again, the enemy was taking ground in my life and my children's life.*

I finally surrendered my will to God, and He released me of the marriage. My children and I were so broken after this, and our son was one month old at the time of our divorce. My question to myself was, "How could I let this happen?"

Transparency

At this point my mind was made up, I don't ever want to be married again, my choice in men is horrible, and my children and I are going to just serve the Lord full force with no looking back. Little did I know, the Lord had a ram in the bush for me. Yes, He did! God is faithful! He blessed me with an amazing man of God who I thought would be the answer to every problem. I remembered the fantasy of having a Prince Charming, my Knight in shining armor, who would come and save the day. He was something I never had before, he was really saved, and I knew in my mind life would be perfect.

We went through pre-marital counseling six months before our wedding and we were so compatible. We came into a covenant with one another to honor the Lord and our marriage by not having sexual relations before our marriage date, and God kept us. I was thinking now I have God's perfect will for my life, and we are going to save the world for Jesus! That was honestly my mindset.

Three months after our wedding day, on Christmas, I found out I was pregnant with our first child. I was so excited and grateful to God for giving us this child. To my surprise, on January 29th, I had a miscarriage. It was horrible and the support I needed and wanted was not there. "God, why did our baby boy die? I finally did everything right and still lost my child? Why Lord?"

Reality Check

After our honeymoon stage in marriage, all hell broke loose. I realized my husband was sarcastic, selfish, had lots of baggage, wanted a domestic Martha Stewart wife, wanted to have numerous children, and believed that the Holy Spirit was of the past, and speaking in tongues was not for today. He was living in the past with a lot of his perspectives and mindsets. He didn't believe a woman could pastor, or minister. There was a lot of mindsets and confusion that came in.

There was a judgmental religious spirit operating that began to suck the life and freedom out of me. I stopped praying in the Spirit out loud throughout my house, I would feel like the children and I were walking on eggshells; I lost my voice and I felt confused about the ministry and calling of God on my life. He was not okay with me going anywhere without him, not even to a store, and he would not work for anyone but God. So, when I say we struggled financially, we struggled financially! Deep rooted rejection and abandonment from my dad and other relationships with men began to spring forth and try to have me wallow in a victim spirit.

Fortification Process

After all this, Holy Spirit took me into a fortification process, which means a defensive wall or other reinforcement built to strengthen a place against attack. The attacks were coming left and right, and the battlefield was in my mind, for the first five to seven years of our marriage. By the time that 2016 got here, I had to make a change. I had to get a God perspective and stop blaming others and having expectations of my husband, wanting love from him that only the Father could give me.

The Lord took me on a journey of healing, mentally, emotionally, physically and spiritually for two years. All the ungodly beliefs I had, and all the spirit soul hurts I encountered, had to be made whole for me to come to a place of peace in my mind, restoration to my husband, and prophetic destiny on my life. God began to slowly take me on a process of understanding where the open door was and how I lost myself in the process of trying to learn how to become a godly wife, who was to submit and care for a house of 16, which we grew to overnight.

God revealed to me that I am my husband's R.I.B., Rest in Brokenness. I was to cover him and be that Proverbs 31 woman who saw it all but prayed him through and pushed him into his destiny and to greatness. My question was, "But Lord, how do I do this?"

<u>Hindsight</u>

The Lord began to show me I was operating in strife, offense, and a people pleasing spirit. I was the victim and my husband was the villain; this was all a lie from the enemy. For two years the Lord took me on a healing journey and plugged me into a powerful ministry of the Word of God, which took me on a Torah journey. I no longer allowed the pain of my past hold me back, or the circumstances of my present-day life.

I had to make a choice to be covered in the dust of my Rabbi Jesus and allow Him to make me whole again. No longer could I blame my husband for anything, instead, God filled him up with the Holy Ghost, filled his heart with the love of Jesus, and gave me a new man. But, had I not made my mind up to renounce making my husband my idol, renouncing rejection, renouncing abandonment, renouncing fear, renouncing depression, and getting healed from the pain of my past, I would not be writing this story today. I realized, no longer was I a victim; I never was a victim, I was always victorious in Christ Jesus who is the author and finisher of my faith.

During this journey, my faith in the God of the impossible was restored; my heart was healed, my mind was healed, my marriage was healed, my children were healing, and my ministry was birthed in January 2019. I know longer said, "Lord rescue me out of the storm and save me from the fire."

Instead I said, "Devil, I am the storm, and Lord Jesus I embrace the fire! Refine me, purge me, cleanse me, make me over again, and mold me into the clay you want me to be."

I learned to evaluate all my relationships and discerned by the grace of God who was really for me and my family, and who was sent on assignment against us. I learned that all the toxicity and negativity that I used to cater to and fuel, I had to repent and start venting to the Lord about all my issues and concerns.

God began to show me the lives of those in the Word of God; Joseph was betrayed and thrown into the pit by his very own brothers before he could reign in the palace, Hadassah had to become Esther before she could be chosen to be Queen Esther and reign in the palace. Ruth had to lose her husband and glean the fields while cleaving to Naomi before she encountered her Boaz, kinsmen redeemer. Peter had to deny Jesus three times before realizing why he was chosen to be the rock the church was built on. Jesus, more than any of these, was betrayed by Judas Iscariot and knew who he was and still showed him unconditional love, all the way to the kiss of betrayal and even the very ones Jesus healed later on said, "CRUCIFY HIM!"

Insight

No longer does the Lord want us to walk around carrying baggage from our past and a casket of dead generational curses. The pain of your past took your innocence, your freedom, your creativity, and your dreams. Through the pain of the bad relationships of your past, it causes a shift and a change in your life's perspective. Nothing can keep you from your destiny, but you! You can prophesy over your own life and kill that voice that speaks to you; it's a generational voice, that talked your mom and/or grandma out of fulfilling their highest destiny and is now coming to speak to you. Break it off in Jesus name!

We serve a mighty God, and sometimes you must wage war against the powers of darkness that come to trip you up and keep you stuck. I'm writing my story and being completely transparent for that little girl inside of you, who lost her way and was violated and striped of her innocence. The little dreamer who gave up on her dream and something died inside of you. The Word of God says to cast down every thought, every vein imagination that tries to exalt itself above the knowledge of God. Shut the mouth of every voice that tells you, you can't do it and tries to talk you out of the very thing God has given you vision to do.

God is not impressed by our titles, degrees, and bank accounts. He looks at our hearts, down on the inside of us, deep down, and is looking for a bride; a remnant who will surrender everything to Him and allow Him to use you for His glory. He's looking for a heart of worship who worships Him in Spirit and in truth. God didn't create you to die spiritually and just to exist. He created you to give your life and life more abundantly. If God allowed something to die in you, it was because He was teaching you something and he has something better or is bringing something within you back to life, through His resurrection power.

Celebrate and welcome every no. The no's come because we were settling, or because God has something better for you that is connected to your yes! Always remember, delayed doesn't mean denied. He said that a man without vision will perish. He gave you a vision because you are the change the world needs to see; your generation needs to see. Don't be afraid, only believe. Remove all doubt and insecurities that come, and toxic relationships. Get away for the unbelief.

Let the little girl in you arise! Arise! It's time to reach back, passed where the pain met you, and embrace the little girl who believed she can, and she did!

Holy Spirit send your fire! Open up the spiritual eyes and ears of my sister reading this chapter. Lord Jesus, awaken her out of her slumber. Give her, her fight back! She is a daughter of the most High

God, a daughter of the King! Lord, open her heart and soul to walk through these next steps.

Action Steps for Your Next Level

1. Repent.

➤ "Repent" literally means being "turn in the other direction" or "again humble" or "penitent." One who is penitent expresses humble or regretful pain or sorrow for sins or offenses. To repent means to come back to yourself, or to that place of humility and sorrow over sin. Come back to the original intent that God ordained for your life before the fall of Adam and Eve. We are coming back to the one who grants forgiveness. We are not trying to do something in our own strength, but connecting our will to the will of God and relying on His strength in our weakness to reverse the curse and forgive us for opening the door. We are reaffirming our need for the Savior, deliverer, and redeemer, Jesus.

2. Renounce.

➤ To "renounce" means to "give up, refuse, or resign by formal declaration." Where repenting is directed toward God, renouncing is directed toward the enemy. We are reversing and revoking any words that contradict God's Word. We are making a formal declaration that we will no longer align ourselves with things that oppose God. We are canceling any and all agreements with the enemy. God has given us authority in Jesus' name to cancel any spiritually binding contracts we may have made with the devil through our words and actions.

Many believers repent of their sins to find themselves losing the battle with the enemy, repeating their failures. We must shut the door on the devil, refusing to walk in the ways of our past.

➤ Renouncing is the means by which we cut off any legal right for Satan to bind or torment us. This is the way we resist him. If our words have been contrary to God's, then we have aligned ourselves with the works of darkness. To be free from them, we must counter those words with God's Word, renouncing hidden works of shame and darkness. "But we have renounced the hidden things of shame, not walking in craftiness or handling the Word of God deceitfully, but by manifestation of the truth commending ourselves to every man's conscience in the sight of God" (2 Cor 4:2).

3. Break.

➤ After we repent, we have the right to cancel or renounce any legal hold the enemy had over us. The yoke of bondage can be broken off our lives. God loves to see us come to the place where yokes are broken! Satan and his demons hate this knowledge. It's common to use anointing oil when praying for someone's deliverance. There is nothing supernatural about the oil. However, it is representing someone who is very supernatural, that one is Jesus, the Messiah, the anointed one (Isaiah 61:1). The oil serves as a point of reference to build faith and make contact.

We are declaring that repentance has taken place, the enemy has been renounced, and now, with the authority of Jesus' name and because of the power of His death and resurrection, the yoke of bondage is broken. "The yoke will be destroyed because of the anointing oil" (Isaiah 10:27). At this point of breaking, a struggle begins and ends. It is the primary place of confrontation with the enemy, and now the light of Jesus is shining where darkness once ruled. The enemy has been found out and cast out. This is a great time of freedom and joy! My husband and I have seen hundreds of people set free by this simple application of God's Word.

4.   Know Your Authority in Jesus Name.

➤ As believers it's critical as we go into battle, beware of your authority in Christ. Deliverance is not a gentle, kind, or friendly activity. We are dealing with disobedient spirits. These demons will use any opportunity to bluff, intimidate, or oppose. I have very little faith in my own ability; however, I know Jesus, and I am convinced that when He said He was giving us authority, He was telling the truth. Always remember the enemy has power but no authority, and the authority of the believer in Jesus trumps the enemy's power. "And these signs will follow those who believe: In My name they will cast out demons; they will speak with new tongues" (Mark 16:17).

➤ We must understand and believe in this authority. It's not haughty authority but a humble, honest, response to who Jesus is and what He has done. In the realm of the spirit, our authority is derived, not from our own strength, but from the one who granted it to us. Our authority is no less because we're new at it or because we're young or frail or not very wise. Spiritual authority depends not upon us but upon Him.

5. Deliverance prayer.

➢ Deliverance prayer is different from our normal prayers, and we may close our eyes and bow our heads, speaking words of encouragement and blessings. When praying deliverance, our eyes are wide open, looking at the one to whom we're ministering, watching for any signs of struggle, sorrow, anger, or other emotions that manifest. Sometimes the demons will try to knock the person out unconscious. Our words are not directed to God; we are launching a head on attack against the enemy. We are coming against whatever demon has deceived and manipulated the one in front of us.

➢ A righteous anger is appropriate when coming against such evil forces. Boldness to confront and put to flight is not out of order. Remember your authority is not in how loud you can be, but in who Jesus is and the finished work on the cross. Volume is not the case but rather a focused and assertive intensity; looking at the enemy in the face and making it clear that you know your authority in Christ and will accept no compromise. The demon must leave now in Jesus name! Remember you have the authority to cast the devil out of your own life and out of the lives of others.

Prayers for Self-Deliverance
& Breaking off Generational Curses

➢ I break all generational curses of pride, rebellion, lust, poverty, witchcraft, idolatry, death, destruction, failure, sickness, infirmity, fear, schizophrenia, and rejection in the name of Jesus.

➢ I command all generational and hereditary spirits operating in my life through curses to be bound and cast out in the name of Jesus.

➢ I command all spirits of lust, perversion, adultery, fornication, uncleanness, sexual imprinting and immorality to come out of my sexual character in the name of Jesus.

➢ I command all spirits of hurt, rejection, fear, anger, wrath, sadness, depression, discouragement, grief, bitterness, and unforgiveness to come out of my emotions in the name of Jesus.

➢ I command all spirits of confusion, forgetfulness, mind control, mental illness, double-mindedness, fantasy, pain, pride, and memory recall to come out of my mind in the name of Jesus.

➢ I break all curses of schizophrenia and command all spirits of double-mindedness, rejection, rebellion and root of bitterness to come out in the name of Jesus.

➢ I command all spirits of guilt, shame, and condemnation to come out of my conscience in the name of Jesus.

➢ I command all spirits of pride, stubbornness, disobedience, rebellion, self-will, selfishness, and arrogance to come out of my will in the name of Jesus.

➢ I command all spirits of addiction to come out of my appetite in the name of Jesus.

➢ I command all spirits of witchcraft, sorcery, divination, masonry, and occult to come out in the name of Jesus.

➢ I command all spirits operating in my head, eyes, mouth, tongue, and throat to come out in the name of Jesus.

➢ I command all spirits operating in my back and spine to come out in the name of Jesus.

➢ I command all spirits operating in my stomach, naval, and

abdomen to come out in Jesus name.

➤ I command all spirits operating in my heart, spleen, kidneys, liver, and pancreas to come out in the name of Jesus.

➤ I command all spirits operating in my sexual organs to come out in the name of Jesus.

➤ I command all spirits operating in my skeletal system, including my bones, joints, knees, and elbows, to come out in the name of Jesus.

➤ I command all spirits operating in my glands and endocrine system to come out in the name of Jesus.

➤ I command all spirits operating in my blood and circulatory systems to come out in Jesus name.

➤ I command all spirits operating in my muscles and muscular system to come out in Jesus name.

➤ I command all religious spirits of doubt, unbelief, error, heresy, and tradition that come in through religion to come out in Jesus name.

➤ I command all spirits from my past that are hindering my present and future to come out in Jesus name.

➤ I command all ancestral spirits that entered through my ancestors to come out in the name of Jesus.

➤ I command all hidden spirits hiding in any part of my life to come out now in the name of Jesus.

➤ I bind all retaliation and back lash from the enemy, the blood of Jesus is against you, and the Lord Jesus rebuke you now in the name of Jesus.

Holy Spirit, I ask you to come in now and fill me up to overflow, every place, baptize me with your all-consuming fire and evidence in speaking in tongues in the name of Jesus! Amen!

Arise, shine; For your light has come! And the glory of the Lord is risen upon you. Isaiah 60:1

Sharlita Monette Barrett

Sharlita Barrett has dedicated her life to serving God, preaching the gospel of Jesus Christ, serving her husband, her children, and humanity. She is the Founder of HIS Love International Ministries, HIS Love Humanitarian Outreach, and Deborah's Arising Women's Ministries. She is devoted to the study of Torah, the prophetic word of the Lord to edify, equip, and train the Body of Christ. She holds a Masters in Hebraic Biblical Studies.

Her love for God and His people has set her on a journey to empower others through revelation on identity in Christ through character refinement. She has overcome many strongholds and obstacles in her life and has learned to embrace the fire and crushing process of the believer. God has kept her for end time ministry and harvest that is quickly approaching now in the end of the age of the Gentiles.

Her life verses are Ephesians 4:11-32, 1 Corinthians 13:4-8, and Matthew 25:*40 "The King will reply, 'Truly I tell you, whatever you did for one of the least of these brothers and sisters of mine, you did for me."*

A DATE WITH DESTINY
Ruth Escarcega

How I Met My Husband

It was the year of January of 1996, a night I was working, but my nephew, Richard, asked me to go out with him and my niece, Yvette, to a club where a co-worker was Dj setting. My nephew knew I was looking for a DJ and felt that this would be a good way to observe his style of entertainment. Before leaving, it was really hard for me to make it out, since I was not used to going to clubs. I decided to go and support my cousin's marriage engagement.

As a single mom of a 5-year-old son, Anthony, I was very strict about not being at out late at night and away from home, but we went to Kelly's Pub in Temple City, California. I didn't go to the bar to meet a man, but little did I know I was going to meet my husband. The first time I went to a club I was quiet and low key observing the fast-moving club scene.

Hindsight from my Husband Point of View

My husband stated that he seen me from across the room and then we made eye contact; he thought, "She likes me."

He told his friend and they thought he was crazy.

He then went to dance with someone else while keeping his eyes on me. After, he asked to buy me a drink and requested to dance. I turned him down and said I didn't drink nor danced.

After the dance ended, he walked over to me and offered me to dance. I turned him down, but my nephew was pushing me to go dance with him. I declined the first time. Then he came back and asked to dance again, so I finally agreed. We danced for two songs.

After we went to sit down and started to conversate. We found out that we had a lot in common, starting with family similarities; we even thought we could be related. I started to feel comfortable and felt more relaxed to socialize. He left for a moment and came back. He then asked me if I could give him a ride home. I was shocked that he asked me, a stranger, for a ride home.

I hesitated and went to tell my nephew, this guy I don't even know is asking me for a ride. Richard said he felt the guy couldn't hurt a fly. So, I give him a ride home. Suddenly I looked around for him and found him outside.

We got in the car, and I told him I had to go over to my niece. I was nervous and was trying to kill time. I went to use the bathroom and lost track of time for 45 minutes. I realized I left the car running with the keys, hoping this guy don't take off with my ride.

Hindsight:

While Gabriel waited for me in the car, I had no idea he was reading my bible in the car. He later shared this with me, as he was reading the bible, he felt God's presence and conviction. He was also in a backslidden state and rededicated his life back God while waiting for her to come back to the car.

I took him home and as I was dropping him off, he offered me to come in to visit. I said, "No, I need to get back home to my son," but, he convinced me to come into his back house and I sit on the couch. His brother came in and introduced himself. Gabriel ended up falling asleep, so I wrote my number down and left my number on the cocktail table.

1st Date: The Miracle Service

Gabriel asked me what I was doing for the weekend. I told him I was going to church and I asked him if he would like to go. Gabriel agreed. We attended the service and he was nervous. He asked God if this was Him. He was contemplating leaving. Eventually he decided to relax and enjoyed the service and departed ways.

The Babysitting Test

One month later, after our miracle service date, I needed a babysitter on a Saturday so I could work. I thought about asking Gabriel to watch my son. I felt I could trust him; so, I asked him to watch my son. He agreed and my son was introduced to his family. The family fell in love with my son, they loved his calm demeanor. My son took a liking to Gabriel, because he bonded well with him. He started developing a connection with my son as a father figure and my son eventually asked to call him dad.

Three months later I met my, soon to be, mother-in-law and other family members. The initial interaction was a bit awkward due to my reserved and shy personality; however, we developed good relationship.

After dating for two years, we had our first biological child. We decided to get married, but it wasn't an easy process. I mentioned the importance of marriage in the eyes of God, but I began to feel resentful about the fact that he did not want to get married. Gabriel felt that marriage was just a piece of paper.

I started praying to God, "If this is the right one for me, let us get married or I am going back home."

One month later, without notice, he said, "Get ready, we are going to get married in two weeks."

We went to Vegas and got married in March 1999.

My First Drink

Later on, my husband scored a high paying job which required many social parties and interactions with clients. I started feeling nervous and experienced social anxiety around the clients. I felt pressure to put on a mask to fit in with the social class. I would never talk or interact with the clients. We went to a Dodgers game and my husband encouraged me to drink. We noticed after drinking, I was relaxed and bubbly. After realizing beer and wine relaxed me, my husband started introducing me to different drinks. Overtime, my husband began to feel concerned about my drinking and demanded me to stop. I was resistant and kept drinking to relax.

The Prophetic Meeting: Deliverance

One year later, I attended a monthly prophetic meeting. Typically, the meetings would be packed, but this month, I was the only person to attend. It was God's divine appointment. The minister prayed and prophesied over me and I begin to experience deliverance from many things.

After the deliverance I felt clean and renewed. I saw my husband and I shared my experience, but he was reluctant to go. Six months later, my husband finally went to the deliverance service and received a prophetic word. The word was powerful and life changing, to the point he stopped drinking, smoking and, other various addictions. My husband immediately started to experience back to back spiritual attacks.

When Gabriel stopped drinking, I saw a different side of my husband. My husband was no longer the happy person, but a dry drunk. His recovery process was so intense I decided to step back and allow God to handle it.

He went to church and no Pastor was able to help him get deliverance. So, my husband started praying at home and listening to sermons.

My Greatest Lessons of Life

I have always had a knowledge of God, and He was always first in my life, but now I have more understanding of who God is and a more developed relationship. My personality has opened up, because the Holy Spirit flows through me. I am more sensitive with the move of God. I am led by the spirit verses the flesh. The Lord has given me my boldness and courage, and I allow God to use me. I learned to let go and allow God to do what he wants to solve my problems. In the past, I worried about my family, but I have developed trust in the Lord.

To the person reading this, no matter where you are in life or what age you are, allow God to be the anchor of your life, no matter what you are going through. Place your trust in Him through the power of prayer. Put forth an everyday communion in prayer. Meditate on these scriptures as you need them, if not daily.

Scriptures References

Psalms 23

The Lord is my shepherd; I shall not want.

He maketh me to lie down in green pastures: he leadeth me beside the still waters.

He restoreth my soul: he leadeth me in the paths of righteousness for his name's sake.

Yea, though I walk through the valley of the shadow of death, I will fear no evil: for thou art with me; thy rod and thy staff they comfort me.

Thou preparest a table before me in the presence of mine enemies: thou anointest my head with oil; my cup runneth over.

Surely goodness and mercy shall follow me all the days of my life: and I will dwell in the house of the Lord forever.

You prepare a table before me in the presence of my enemies. You anoint my head with oil; my cup overflows.

Surely your goodness and love will follow me all the days of my life, and I will dwell in the house of the Lord forever.

Scriptures References

Psalms 23

He that dwelleth in the secret place of the most High shall abide under the shadow of the Almighty. I will say of the Lord, He is my refuge and my fortress: my God; in him will I trust. Surely he shall deliver thee from the snare of the fowler, and from the noisome pestilence. He shall cover thee with his feathers, and under his wings shalt thou trust: his truth shall be thy shield and buckler. Thou shalt not be afraid for the terror by night; nor for the arrow that flieth by day; Nor for the pestilence that walketh in darkness; nor for the destruction that wasteth at noonday. A thousand shall fall at thy side, and ten thousand at thy right hand; but it shall not come nigh thee. Only with thine eyes shalt thou behold and see the reward of the wicked. Because thou hast made the Lord, which is my refuge, even the most High, thy habitation; There shall no evil befall thee, neither shall any plague come nigh thy dwelling. For he shall give his angels charge over thee, to keep thee in all thy ways. They shall bear thee up in their hands, lest thou dash thy foot against a stone. Thou shalt tread upon the lion and adder: the young lion and the dragon shalt thou trample under feet. Because he hath set his love upon me, therefore will I deliver him: I will set him on high, because he hath known my name. He shall call upon me, and I will answer him: I will be with him in trouble; I will deliver him, and honour him. With long life will I satisfy him, and shew him my salvation.

Ruth Escarcega

Ruth Escarcega is Co-Pastor of Open Heaven Ministries, alongside her Husband, Pastor Gabriel Escarcega.

RUTH ESCARCEGA

FEAR NOT, I AM WITH YOU
Derrie Davis

W hat do we know about fear? I know fear is merely <u>F</u>alse <u>E</u>vidence <u>A</u>ppearing <u>R</u>eal. I've also heard that fear makes us <u>F</u>orget <u>E</u>verything <u>A</u>nd <u>R</u>un, and I have wanted to do that many times. But God gave me a better understanding, He told me with FEAR, you must <u>F</u>ace <u>E</u>very <u>A</u>dversity <u>R</u>igorously, so here I am.

I've vowed and I'm determined to get out of my comfort zone and out of my own way. I've decided to let go and let God! I'm going up against the enemy of fear today! I'm writing this afraid. So now, let's talk about fear.

Fear is debilitating. Fear will cause us to stay stagnant. It will cause the smallest situation to appear so monumental. Fear will have you seeing things that are not real. Fear will have you conjure up an entire scenario in your mind that never existed and never will.

Fear has stopped my progress in so many areas of my life. Fear began to grip me at a very young age. It started when my mom began to lose her mind. My grandma said at about the age of 28, she could see a change in my mom. My mom began not caring about herself. She started walking around barefooted, and she stopped caring about her appearance. She would come and go with different men, and she became an alcoholic. I was told my mom smoked lots of weed; later on, in life, I found out that she was using crack.

Sounds like fear had gripped her and she was anesthetizing herself, because of whatever pain and trauma she was experiencing. My mom ended up in a mental institution called Camarrillo and then, on Skid Row. I was able to visit her from time to time.

We were living in South Central Los Angeles in the Imperial Courts Projects. I was about 5 years old and my brother, Gregory, was 2 years old. My mom had 4 children in total, but only my brother Greg and I lived with my mom at this time.

I remember being very hungry, going in and out of the refrigerator. I would eat crackers, pickles, bread, and anything that I could find. My mom left me and my brother home alone about 3-5 days. She wasn't around my family a lot after she became ill. Most of the time, they didn't even know what was going on in our lives.

I believe my mom would leave us alone regularly, but this particular time she just never came back. Someone eventually called the authorities and told them that we were home alone and abandoned, so the police came to pick us up. I remember being wrapped and taken away in plaid blankets. It's still a vivid picture in my mind.

We were taken to a place called McClaren Hall. This was a place where abused & abandoned children are taken and later picked up by family members or put into foster care. I was told that I was so hungry when we arrived at McClaren Hall, I snatched another little girl's sandwich and gobbled it down.

None of our family members came to pick us up. So, my brother and I ended up as orphans. We were eventually taken into foster care. I believe this is when I really became fearful.

My foster mom's name was Ms. Banks. I still remember her name, and I can still see her face. She was very mean and abusive. She abused me physically and mentally. I became extremely scared, terrified, and withdrawn; I was with this person that was not only a stranger, but she also terrified me. I felt some sort of hate and anger coming from her spirit.

My family eventually found out that my brother and I were taken away and placed in foster care. They knew that we were placed in Compton, but they didn't know the exact location. They began trying to locate us. My aunt had a conversation with a co-worker, telling her that my brother and I were placed in foster care somewhere in Compton. By change, her co-worker happened to live in Compton and had a neighbor who was a foster parent.

My aunt described us to her co-worker, and she told my aunt to come by and see if her neighbors foster children was us, because the description my aunt gave of us looked and sounded familiar. My aunt came to check, and it was us playing in the back yard. That's was all God who led my aunt to find us.

I was so terrified and afraid of my foster mom. She damaged my self-esteem. I had such a poor self-image after I left her home. One reason was because I was given to a complete stranger who was abusing me, and second, I was abandoned by both my parents; because of this, I never felt worthy or good enough. The very people who were supposed to protect me were not there!

After my brother and I were located, my grandmother and aunt started going to court hearings. They were first given visitation rights and then my grandma gained legal custody of us. I was 6 years old then.

My mom's family wasn't the best family either, but unfortunately you can't choose your family. They were very harsh and hard hearted. At one point I found myself slipping into that mindset. They were all bitter, negative and angry. We lived in poverty and we didn't have much. Every day was a struggle for us.

My family also aided in my poor self-image. They'd look down and frown upon someone who had a healthy self-image. If you felt good about yourself, said or thought you were beautiful, or thought highly of yourself you were labeled as conceited and stuck on yourself, and they would do their best to tear you down. I always had to shrink who I was when I was around my family for the fear of them accusing me of being stuck up.

The more that I look back, most of my family had low self-esteem too. I'm now realizing that they couldn't teach or give me what they didn't have. This type of thinking and suppression made me go completely into a shell. It made me feel uncomfortable around people, and I felt like I couldn't be myself. I always felt I would be ridiculed if I thought highly if myself, so I'd downplay my beauty and all of my great qualities.

I had the lightest complexion in my family, so I was often called whitey or white girl. I was often told that I thought I was better because of my fair skin. I was told that I would get a job before a dark-skinned person. This kind of talk really made me feel like an outcast and like I didn't belong.

This was very hard for me to process. 5 years ago, I found out, through a DNA test, that the person listed on my birth certificate as my father, Eugene Davis, was not my dad. My dad's name is Marvin Ray King, and he was in fact Caucasian. He was a Vietnam Vet who committed suicide in prison when he was 47 years old. I don't even think he ever knew I existed, but to God be the glory, that I was able to find out this information.

Finding out who my father was gave me some closure. I was able to talk to some of his relatives. These findings also gave me some understanding as to why I looked different and verified that I wasn't just some freak of nature.

I had a hard time expressing myself because of the fear that gripped me. I quickly became a people pleaser, because I didn't want to be rejected like I had been in the past. Because of the fear of rejection and the people pleasing spirit that gripped me, I found myself in situations that weren't the best for me. I was in and out of relationship, one after another, with guys. I was looking for love in all the wrong places. I just wanted someone to truly love and care for me.

I was looking for love from a man, because I needed that father figure. I was also looking for love from a mother figure. I had a yearning for the voids to be filled in my life from an external source that only God could fill internally.

<u>Hindsight 20/20</u>

Looking back at my life, I would not change a thing. I realize God has me right where I need to be at this very moment. If I hadn't gone through what I went through, I wouldn't be who I am today. Little did I know, God had been with me the whole time.

I'd often ask God why I couldn't have my parents in my life. I'd feel sad sometimes when Mother and Father's Day would come around. What God placed in my spirit is that, had I been raised with my parents I would not be the parent that I am today. He said that I would have turned out as someone totally different.

I once told God, even before I had children, if he would help me and keep me in my right mind, I'd make sure I would never abandon my children or leave them in the hands of someone else to raise. I told Him I would be the best parent that I could be, with His help, and He's been faithful and has done just what I've asked. He is my Abba Father. He is my daddy.

So, the Lord gave me a double blessing, I have twins, Devin and Damion, a girl and a boy 34 years old. I have a 13-year-old son, Aulton, whom I was married to his dad. I didn't seek God before marring him, and it didn't work out. I have 2 grandchildren, Onyx who is 4 years old and Dakota who is 1 years old. I'm so proud of my little family.

Had I not gone through rejection and abandonment I would not have sought God for His acceptance. I've discovered that He's a mother to the motherless and a father to the fatherless; on top of all that, He calls me His friend, and he accepts me no matter what.

I don't have to please God. He's already pleased with me through His son Jesus. There's nothing that I can do or not do that will change His love and acceptance for me. God is Love. His very being and essence is Love, and He's in love with me, and you.

He didn't want me trusting and putting my faith in a man or woman for my security and validation. That's why I couldn't get comfortable in a relationship with anyone, where I was looking for them to do only what God could do. I would have been searching a lifetime for fulfillment and satisfaction. God is faithful and he'll never let us down. He wants the ultimate relationship with us.

God wanted me to stay humble so that I could help lift other's self-esteem. God has imbedded something so strong in me. I love to give compliments. I've always been that way ever since I was a little girl, as young as 6 years old. I would be in the grocery, out and about, giving compliments and finding beauty in others. God always puts it on my heart to look for an opportunity to uplift someone else.

It lifts me to lift other people! I feel like I'm truly giving when I can reinforce and highlight the great qualities that God has blessed others with. It truly gives me joy! I've learned to see the beauty in everything.

Although these experiences were traumatic for me, God will use my mess as a message to help heal and free others for His Glory. Hindsight is that I have naturally become an encourager. I'm so conscious and careful to give encouragement at all costs. I've been humbled and deem it imperative, because I lacked the encouragement and validation that I so longed to receive from family and those that I looked up to. The devil meant it for evil and for it to destroy me, but God meant it for my good.

So, the fear that you and I have felt for so long is just the enemy's tactic to keep us stagnant and paralyzed. He's always rearing his ugly head to keep us from perusing our purpose and plan that God has for our lives, from the beginning, before we were placed in our mothers wound. The enemy wants us distracted. From here on out, I'm stepping and stomping on the head of the enemy of fear!

For God has not given us the spirit of fear but one of love
and of power and of a sound mind. 2 Timothy 1:7
God said, "Fear not for I am with you."

MEET THE WRITER

Derrie Davis

CONFUSION TO CLARITY
Margo Williams

As I sit and ponder over my life, I see years of confusion. The interesting part of this, is I didn't know that I was confused. That path that I was walking was a dark road. The company that I kept was a sure-fire way to a short-lived life. The individuals did not motivate me or speak life. My focus was on what man thought, and not what God desired. I knew of God, but I didn't know Him personally.

Knowing God personally is experiencing His deep mysteries. Once He removes the blinders off your eyes, you'll be able to have a keen ability to see what He shows you and hear what He's speaking in the spirit. This walk we're on, is a faith walk till the end. It requires spending intentional quiet time, prayer time, and worship time. Yes, this is a choice, once we come into the understanding.

For years I thought I was confident, but once I met my child's father, this quickly changed. The abuse I received was on different levels and became physical in the second trimester of my pregnancy. I was called names until it broke my spirit. This is what the abuser does to tear others down. Once they tear you down spiritually, threats and physical abuse become the norm.

I had such low self-esteem; I ate to feel good, not realizing that I had gone from a size 15 to size 34 women in less than 2 years. The name calling increased, because he was embarrassed to be seen with me. This was one of the most confusing times of my life. I couldn't understand what I did wrong. I had a child with this person, but did not experience joy, nor was I treated respectfully.

But one day my eyes were opened, and I met someone who told me that I was worth more, I was beautiful, and deserved better. No, this didn't occur within a church, but this was God's way of saying "*Walk away.*" This was only the beginning of God getting my attention.

70

Now, I want to be the one to encourage another victim of abuse, or someone suffering from low self-esteem. Know that God has greater for you and wants you to experience peace and joy. You're not just living to exist, but there is a magnificent purpose attached to your life.

How Precious You are in the Eyes of God

In the book of Ephesians 1, verses 4-5, it reads in the KJV:

4) According as he hath chosen us in him before the foundation of the world, that we should be holy and without blame before him in love:

5) Having predestined us unto the adoption of children by Jesus Christ to himself, according to the good pleasure of his will.

As you can see, we all are created with a purpose. God knew us before now, and His plans were already in place. Along with us walking in His purpose, is us allowing Him to get pleasure from His divine design. There is so much we have not yet seen; this is why we are to rely on His perfect plan.

Our protection is in the will of God. We may go through life situations, but His hand is upon you. It doesn't matter what anyone says or think about you. The way you look is special, because your design is divine.

The book of Ephesians 2, verse 10, KJV, reads:

10) For we are the workmanship, created in Christ Jesus unto good works, which God hath before ordained that we should walk in them.

How We Become Caught up
in Situations that Blindside Us

The company we choose to spend time with can determine our future. I'm speaking from a lesson well learned. I had to bump my head numerous times, but I'm sharing this now to help prevent another person from making poor decisions.

In the book of Proverbs 13, verse 20, KJV, it reads:

> *20) He that walketh with wise men shall be wise: but a companion of fools shall be destroyed.*

The individuals we allow in our space will play a major role in our lives. Take everything into prayer, including those you allow in your life. Pray their names to God and wait for Him to reveal. The revelation can come in many ways, including through a situation. Ask God to remove those who are hindrances in your life.

In the book of Proverbs 14, verse 27, KJV, it reads:

> *14) Peace I leave with you, my peace I give unto you: not as the world giveth, give I unto you. Let not your heart be troubled, neither let it be afraid.*

The Word of God is very direct and intentional in the messages that God wants us to understand. Peace is a blessing from God, and He wants us to dwell in it. For many years, I lived in chaos, and peace was far from me. It wasn't until I fully surrendered, that I can truly say I understand what Peace feels like.

I gave into the Will of God, and began to study the Holy Bible, and commune with Him. This does not happen overnight, but it is a process we all must go through. So, if you are new in learning, know that maturing is continual as you study the Holy Bible, and seek God personally. The Word of God is like a navigator and is full of directions.

In the Book of John 14, verse 26, KJV, it reads:

> *26) But the Comforter, which is the Holy Ghost, whom the Father will send in my name, he shall teach you all things, and bring all things to your remembrance, whatsoever I have said unto you.*

Know this! – The Word of God will not fail you, but man can! This is why it's important to know how our Heavenly Father speaks, and when He speaks. Your clarity is with knowing how you're being directed from day to day. However you are directed, it's better on the journey God has planned for you. But remember, after all is said and done, it's for His glory. Continually fix your eyes straight ahead, and you will not go down the wrong path.

I pray that each of you will come into the knowledge of who God is.

Read, use as a prayer, and meditate on Ephesians 1, verses 17-19, KJV:

> *17) That the God of our Lord Jesus Christ, the Father of glory, may give unto you the spirit of wisdom and revelation in the knowledge of him:*
> *18) The eyes of your understanding being enlightened; that ye may know what is the hope of his calling, and what is the riches of the glory of his inheritance in the saints:*
> *19) And what is the exceeding greatness of his power to us- ward who believe, according to the working of his mighty power.*

May you all be blessed beyond measure.

Margo Williams

Margo Williams is the author of, "When God Speaks, Poems and Prayers," and "I Am Divinely Designed," an interactive children's book. She is known for her love of writing, photography, Advocacy/Education of Domestic Violence, Rape Crisis Intervention, Human Trafficking; Coaching, and Public Speaking.

As a Minister and a prophetess, Margo's mission is to be effective in every God given assignment. She desires to see every individual whom she cross paths with, to know God and His purpose for their lives.

Margo is currently a Behavior Interventionist and has worked in the field of Human Services, within many communities over the years and has gained experience working with at-risk youth in foster care, Autistic/blind individuals, teen parents, and as a behavior interventionist.

NEVER ALONE
Jessica D.K. Romero

Jeremiah 29:11

"For I know the thoughts I think of you", said the Lord.
"Thoughts of good and not of evil, to give you a future and a
hope"

Life Growing Up

As a child I felt like I never belonged. My father took me, my brother, and sister from our mom in California, and took us to New Mexico. He wrote a letter saying he would return us to her in two weeks. At one point, my mother had a bad feeling; something didn't feel right. She made a plan to come to New Mexico and reunite with my dad, pretending to work things out only as a means to get us back to California.

My mother did get us back, only for my father to kidnap us and take us back New Mexico. My mother was only able to get my brother and sister back because he refused to give me back, so I was left behind.

In the process of trying to get me back, my mother did in fact go to jail for trying to take me back to California with her. This is where things began to get chaotic in my life. The loneliness sank in and I was kept away from all family.

Whenever my cousins went on vacation, I was always left behind. I was never given a reason why I couldn't go; I just couldn't go. I was an only child growing up. This made it hard for anyone to see what was going on behind closed doors.

My father was an alcoholic and addicted to drugs. He drank, smoked, and shot up anything that was in front of him. When he would pass out, I would sneak out the house and go down the street to a couple of older lady's houses.

One of the ladies taught me how to pick, boil, and jar peaches. The other lady showed me how to crochet. By the time we were done, it was dark out and I was scared to go back home, worried my father would be awake. I'd hurry back home to find him still passed out. Whew! What a relief that was.

I remember rolling his cigarettes for him at the age of 7. This is also the age I became homeless for the first time, two days too long. My father said he kicked me out to teach me a lesson. What lesson could a 7-year-old possibly learn?

At the age of 9, I "graduated" to rolling marijuana. One day I decided to keep one of his rolled joints and sneak a beer behind my grandma's house and test it out for myself. It's then when I discovered why everyone around me was laughing and having a good time.

They were not always happy. As a matter as a fact, there was plenty of fighting with bats, chains, and whatever was around to win the battle.

At a very young age I remember the beatings and different men coming in and out of my room (uncles, cousins, friends of the family, my dad and even people I didn't know). Smoking cigarettes, marijuana, and drinking became a habit for me as well. I started drinking and smoking before, during, and after the men would come in and out of my room. Realizing it took away the physical, emotional, and mental pain I was going through.

I had to skip school, quiet often, until broken bones and bruises were healed. I was asked by a school councilor why I was missing so much school or what happened to my face, arm, legs etc… My answer was always, "I fell" or "I was sick."

When it came to tests at the end of the school year, I flunked the

4th grade because I didn't have the knowledge it took to pass the test. My father picked me up from school the day I got my report card. When he opened it and saw that I flunked, he got extremely mad. Needless to say, when we got home, I got the beating of a lifetime. My father told me that I had embarrassed him!

Two things I hated growing up, my last name and my birthdate. I cried often; whenever I was alone and would say out loud, "I wish I was not born a Romero." I hated my birthdate, because I was brought into a world that I hated.

I can honestly say I only have one good memory of me and my father. This was when I held on to his belt loops from behind while I skated on the ice in the wintertime. I was always around men and never had anyone to play with. I was not allowed to play with toys; I was too busy entertaining, cooking, and cleaning.

I often went to bed without dinner and there was plenty of food in the house. If I cried or yelled while a man entered my room, I went to bed without dinner. If I didn't cook fast enough or spilled the beer while I was serving him and his friends, I went to bed without dinner.

I came home 5 minutes late and my father was waiting for me. As I reached the 3rd step of our trailer, he came out with a broom. I got scared and turned around to run, but he was too quick and swung at my back. The broom broke as I fell to the ground. He said if I continued to cry, he would give me something to cry about. He picked me up by my hair and pulled me inside.

When we got inside, he told me to go get my baby chick that I had been raising. I did as he said. When I handed him my baby chick, he broke its neck right in front of me. I tried so hard not to cry, because I didn't want another beating. He then put the dead baby chick in my hands and told me to go throw it in the trash outside.

Another time, he punched me on my nose. I couldn't eat my spaghetti because it was too hot for me. My nose started to bleed, and he made me go to the bathroom and get my own toilet paper to clean myself up. He wanted to go somewhere, but could not until I was done eating. So that night I went to bed without eating.

I raised myself, I taught myself how to cook, clean, and all other things an adult (parent) is supposed to do or help a child with. I did feel important doing adult things, because it seemed that was the only time one or two people acknowledged me.

While being high or drunk, my dad would go into my room and urinate in the corner, leaving me to clean it up, yet the smell lingered. I had to babysit my three-year-old and one-year old cousins while he my uncle and aunty went to dance and party at the City Hall. I remember being frightened, holding my cousins tightly close to me in my arms, wishing someone was there to protect us.

As time went on the men continued to come in and out at all hours of the day and night, never understanding what or why it was going on.

There have been many more incidents growing up, and I thought it was normal until 1988 when a school councilor asked me again, "What was going on."

I could not contain myself and broke down crying. We sat there for a couple of hours talking and hugging. A little while later a social worker from Child Protected Service came in and I had to only repeat a little of what I told the school counselor. The social worker tells me to get in her car and we headed to my house.

Long story short, that would be the last time I saw my father; he was arrested, and I became a ward of the state at age 12. This is when

I learned I was a survivor of child trafficking. Not clear at all what that meant until I became an adult.

I was scared to tell anyone the truth about what was going on at home. I felt if I would have said something sooner, I would not have gone through as much as I did. I was scared of my father and what he would do if I told on him and the others; therefore, I kept silent for such a long time.

I learned it is not ok to keep quiet. I was also lying about what was going on behind closed doors. I was protecting those who had been committing a heinous crime. Whether scared or not, I allowed others to continue those acts. Since then, anything that is not going according to how I believe is should be or if things are not going well, I speak up.

I stand up for what is right, and I stand up for those who are not able to. I was able to get out of my situation, because I finally spoke up. My father went to jail for a short amount of time and all the others got away with a clean slate.

My family in California knew what was going on, but they didn't know what to do. My father's side of the family seemed to be upset about my dad going to jail and giving a bad name to the family. To me, I didn't care what they thought, because they didn't do anything for me when I was in need.

Life as an Adolescent

My first stop was University of New Mexico Mental Health for roughly 6 months. I was prescribed medication and sedated at times. I was found a foster home, where I would be mistreated. From there, I went to live with an aunt. One of the monster's that would come into my room in the middle of the night lived there.

Another nightmare in the making was at my auntie's. Her husband committing sexual acts at my bedside while he assumed I was asleep. I told my social worker about this and instantly, I was removed and was placed in a group home.

In this group home, I made a couple of "Friends" who were as troubled as I was. We would sneak out late and sneak back in even later, drunk or high. By this time, I was a very angry and rebellious adolescent, thinking the world owed me. If I didn't get my way I would run. It made things easier for me, or at least I thought it did.

At the age of 14, I walked down unknown streets with nowhere to go; glancing at houses, smelling either food cooking or laundry being done, wishing I lived a normal life and wanting desperately to be inside one of those houses. The family that lived inside had to be better than the one I grew up with, definitely better than being on the streets alone, cold, and hungry.

As I began to walk down a main street, a red truck pulls over and asks me if I want to party? With nowhere to go, free liquor, and some company, I hopped in the truck quickly. We drove up the Sandia Mountains. On the way up there, one of the guys sat in the bed truck with me. I remember guzzling down a fifth of Jack Daniels and some beer, wanting to look and be grown, driving fast through windy and steep roads, giggling and laughing along the way.

Honestly, there's not much I remember about the ride up there, or the ride down. I would be awake one moment and the next passed out! The next time I woke up I felt my body being picked up and hearing guys talk. When I opened my eyes, I was in the doorway outside of an emergency room. Once I came to, a nurse came to check on me and said I had been asleep for nearly two days. I had IV's and a catheter. I knew if I didn't get out of there, soon my caseworker would show up and send me to another group home or to an institution.

I tried to pull out the catheter so I can get out of there as quickly as possible. As I'm tugging on the catheter, a nurse comes in and says, "Stop or you will pull out your insides!"

I said "No, I have to get out of here!"

I kept on tugging and tugging but would feel a sharp pain every time. A couple of minutes later a few nurses came in and gave me a shot to calm me down. As I'm feeling woozy, the nurses put me in wrists and ankles restraints. My caseworker was called and was told I was awake and trying to leave.

When she got there, she looked at me with such a saddened and disappointed look. I cried and asked her to get me out of there. She told me they had to observe me a bit longer, because I had alcohol poisoning. I had no choice but to give in. Once released from the hospital, I was placed in another group home. I didn't stay long as usual. When things got tough, I got going. So again, I ran away to what was familiar, the streets.

When I ran away from the group home, I got caught pretty quickly, just like all the other times. I never lasted long on the streets. This time the police took me to juvenile hall. This was a whole new world to me. It definitely wasn't something I was interested in. Screaming is all I heard once I was booked in. I was taken directly to my cell.

The food was pretty good, because I had not been eating well, but as days went by, the food became less and less tasteful. We had three-minute showers and a lot of naked bodies, yet I was still embarrassed to shower with other females. Even if we were not done, the water was cut off, soap and all.

The boys and girls were able to communicate, meaning we went to lunch together, had television time together, and was able to go to the yard and chill with one another.

Arts and crafts were my favorite activities. It was something I was good at and it took my mind off of being locked up behind steel doors and cold cement walls. I got really close to one of the guards. She treated me like a human being. At times she snuck me home cooked food, snacks, and fresh fruit. These were the things that we did not get while in Juvi. She always told me, "One day everything will be ok," and she said it with a smile.

I would get angry quite often and have episodes (fits). During one of those fits I bit her on her arm. It's not something I planned, I was trying to get away from those who were holding me down and her arm happened to be in my face. A few days later she came back to work and showed me the bite on her arm, and I gasped. It looked horrible.

"Because of you I cannot even hold my baby."

I said I was sorry, but she didn't want to hear anything I had to say. She was not going to accept my apology. As days went on, she kept ignoring me and wouldn't even look my way. I would cry and tell her how sorry I was, but she didn't care and never did accept my apology.

One day the guard said, "You have a visit."

"A visit!" I never got visits. No one cared about me enough to come see me, or so I thought. As I'm being walked down the hall and into the visiting room, I see my caseworker. She was a really sweet woman, who in fact really cared about me. She always did her best to make sure I ate, had clothes, and a warm place to sleep. She tried to do what she could for me when she could.

I ran up to her and gave her a huge hug. She asked me how I was doing and told me that it was really nice to see me. I told her it was really nice to see her. I also told her that I was okay, just tired of being there.

She told me she had some good news. She said I was being released that day. She brought me some new clothes and shoes. I changed out and then she took me to eat. After we ate, I asked her where I was going. She said back to University of New Mexico Mental Health. Hey, anything was better than Juvi.

I didn't like University of New Mexico Mental Health, because I was always zombied out on medication. The doctors tried many, many, different kinds of medication. Most of them had a lot of side effects that made me really uncomfortable like unwanted body movements, dry mouth, restlessness, always feeling tired, dizziness and many more. The only one I really liked were the ones that kept me asleep at night.

I got into a lot of trouble for being disrespectful and not obeying staff or rules. So, while others were having a good time watching a movie or off campus activities, I was in my room alone. It's like as if I didn't know how to get along with others and I didn't want to take orders from authority. My mentality was, "I raised myself, so why should I have to listen to anyone?"

At one point, I was on a good streak with good behavior, but that never lasted long. My attitude always got in the way. One day my case manager asks me if I knew where my biological mother was. I told her the last thing I heard; she was living in California. A few weeks went by and I was called into the office. "We got some great news; we found your mother!"

I became really excited and started to cry. They asked me if I wanted to meet her and I said yes. It was still going be a month or so until the court approved the visit. I didn't know anything about my mother. I was always told what a horrible person she was and how she never wanted me. So naturally, I believed what they told me.

My entire life, I had resentment towards my mother. Asking myself, "Why was I the one she didn't want... Why this? Why that? Why me?"

The accusations about her didn't matter to me anymore. I didn't care! I was going to have a family! I was going to have a mom. A mom I always wanted. I remember when I was about 7 or 8 years old, packages would come in the mail with my name on it. I would ask my father about it and all he would say is, "I'm sending them back."

Later on, I found out that they were Christmas and birthday gifts from my mom. The case manager also told me that I had two brothers and two sisters. Wow! This was the greatest news of my life. I was finally going to have a family that I had longed for.

In the meantime, I was getting letters from my brothers and sisters. Arrangements were made and my mom came down to Albuquerque, New Mexico. She went to court to receive custody of me. Plane tickets were bought, and I was on my way to Barstow, California.

As we flew into Ontario I fell in love with the scenery. These huge tall palm trees that looked like fireworks exploding, were all over the place. There were lights everywhere; huge buildings that also had lights around and on them. I LOVE LIGHTS, any type of lights! When I see lights, I'm in a trance.

By the time we got to California it was dark out. I was a little nervous and shy the entire drive, which made the drive seemed really short. I was worried what my brothers and sisters would think of me. I did feel like an outsider because I've never met or talked to them before.

As soon as I entered the door to my mom's apartment, my little brother wrapped his body around my leg. My sisters greeted me in a loving way and my other brother, well he's not one to jump when something exciting is going on.

Things were going well. I started junior high. I was being a good child I started getting the grasp of what it was like to have a family. Then my attitude started, I began to skip school and drinking Jack Daniels and smoking weed again.

During one of my ditching sessions, I met this young girl around my age, 14, and an older guy in his 30's. They had been smoking out of a can and had offered me some. Of course, I said yes, so the young girl demonstrated how I need to do it. I asked what it was, and she said crack. I really didn't know what it was, but I tried it anyways. She told me not to hold it in too long because my heart can explode. I was not sure if it was true or not, so I did as she said.

After I blew out the smoke my heart began to race, my hands shook, and I felt stuck in one position. As much as I didn't like the feeling, I wanted more, my mouth was craving it. I was too embarrassed to ask for more because they didn't offer. The guy started to get hostile so the young girl told me it would be a good idea to leave. I didn't think to ask if she was going to be okay, I just bolted out the door with a racing heart and a confused mind.

After about 15 minutes I calmed down and went to my mom's husband's sisters to ask her if she would smoke a joint with me. She let me in, and I told her what happened, then she smoked with me. I smoked a lot of marijuana and got really high and then realized the time. I was skipping school and needed to be home on time as if I went to school.

When I got home my mom was gone, but my older sister was there and, instantly, she knew I was high. I ended up passing out and when

I woke up, I was in the bedroom closet. What I was doing in there, I have no clue.

After about six months of continuous ditching, drinking, coming home late, sneaking out, and getting high, my mom thought it would be a good idea to send me to live with my older sister in Long Beach. I moved in with an uncle, a cousin, and my sister.

Long Beach was much faster than Barstow, more action and violence. Every time I heard gun shots, I ran outside to see what was going on. My sister would yell at me from the second-floor window telling me to come inside, "Are you stupid?" so, inside I'd go.

On a Saturday afternoon I went down to do some laundry and two girls about my age were giving me the stank eye, so I gave the stank eye back. I put the laundry to wash and I was walking out the laundry room when one of the girls started talking nonsense and cursed at me. All I remember was that I challenged her. I went upstairs to tell my sister what was going on and she gave me her class ring to put on and fight with.

On my way down the stairs, I'm yelling at her telling her to meet me in the alley. As my sister and I, along with the two girls, walk into the alley, we instantly began to fight. At first, she was on top of me, then I rolled her over and I was on top. I started hitting her in her face time after time. My sister had to pull me off her while I was still swinging. My sister said, "That's enough."

We went upstairs, but as I began to calm down, we heard a knock on the door. My sister looked out the window and said there were five older girls and the two young ones. My sister said I better handle it outside. As I opened the door the older girls started yelling and cursing at me, "Look at what you did."

I saw the girls face that I fought, and she had lumps covering her face. I told them "She started with me, so we fought."

Next, the sister of the girl I fought pushed me through the kitchen window and it shattered. The older girls then picked me up by my feet and hung me upside down over the balcony. I yelled at the top of my lungs, "Drop me, I don't care, I'll die instantly anyways."

I repeated it over and over again with no fear at all of dying. "Do you want to die, do you?"

Again, I yelled, "Drop me, drop me!"

They pulled me up and threatened me, if I ever come near her sister again, they were going to kill me. Me being the stubborn and mouthy adolescent that I was, I said, "I'll be waiting." I never heard from them again.

I wanted to be grown and do grown folks' things, like hang out with my sister, drink, and party. One day my sister took me with her to a party and introduced me to a guy name Spider, who was in a gang. As the party went on, Spider invited me to go on a walk. I declined the invite, but my sister told me to go with him. To be honest I didn't want to be an adult anymore. I was scared to go for a walk in the dark with a 25-year-old. Remember I was only 14 years old.

I ended up going on this walk with him. The entire time he talked about how he was in a gang and how at any moment we could be shot. The people who wanted him dead didn't care who was around, they would get shot too. The walk we were taking seemed long, and being that I was scared, it seemed like an eternity.

As we got closer, I saw that we were going to a park, so I headed over to the benches. He had a different idea; he pulled me into the park bathroom and raped me. Before I could even get my pants up, he was gone. He left me there alone. After I got dressed, I walked to the nearest main street to see if I knew where I was, and nope, not even close; I had no idea where I was.

I started to cry more than I was before. I was looking back and forth, wondering which way to go when a car pulled up. I jumped not knowing who they were or what could happen. The passenger window rolled down and it was an older couple, "Are you alright sweetie?"

I replied with, "No I'm lost and don't know how to get home."

"Well don't you have someone you can call?"

"I'm not sure, my sister is at a party and I... I," the words were hard to form, but they eventually came out, "And I just got raped."

The older woman gasped and asked me where I lived. I gave her the address and she knew exactly where it was. They both told me to get in the car and they would take me home. Without thinking or making a conscious decision, I got in the back seat feeling embarrassed, shaken, and scared. When we got closer to my sister's place, I began to recognize the area and I shouted, "There it is, that's it right there!"

They asked if I was sure and I said yes. I got out the car, thanked them and went inside. When I knocked on the door my sister answered and asked where I had been. When I told her what happened, she didn't believe me.

"I'm telling you the truth," I cried.

That situation was never brought up again. I don't know the conversation between my mother and sister, but I was right back in Barstow living with my mom. A few months later I got sick and kept vomiting, my mom decided to take me to the doctors. I rode in the bed of the truck, and most of the way I was vomiting.

We checked in, I did some tests, and waited for the doctor to come in. As he came in, he gave us my results. "Miss Romero, you're 3 1/2 months pregnant."

I didn't understand or know what to think. Growing up, nobody told me I was going to have a period; there were no birds and the bee's conversation. So, I shrugged it off, still not comprehending what was going on.

As time went by my breasts began to grow drastically, as well as my stomach, I was not able to fit into any of my clothes. One day my mom tells me that I'm going back to New Mexico. Next thing my clothes are packed and I'm back on a plane. I go to live with an aunt of mine. After about a month of being there. I began getting sharp pains in my stomach. My aunt rushed me to the hospital and they immediately started to poke and probe me. It turned out my baby was ready to come; by this time, I was 5 1/2 months along.

They stop the contractions and sent me home with medicine. I had to keep injecting myself in my thigh and I had a machine that monitored the baby. I went to home school, but that didn't last long, because my home-schooling teacher was a man and my aunts boyfriend began to get jealous. So that was that.

A month later I began feeling the pains again and started crying at the top of my lungs. My aunt was in the bathroom, so I had to go to her because she was not paying any attention to me. I told her what was going on and she called my doctor. He said I was contracting 13 times per minute, so get me to the hospital as quick as she could.

The medicine was not helping. I'm a fifteen-year-old and about to have a baby. On the way to the hospital, my aunt stopped at my uncle's house for who knows what. On the way there she was not being careful going over potholes or bumps and was driving recklessly.

Every time she went over the potholes, I scream because the pain got worse. We finally got to the hospital and I was put on a gurney and wheeled into an unknown room. The nurse begins to put an IV in and ask me if I wanted pain medicine. I said "No"! I didn't want my baby to be exposed to that.

As time went on the pains got worse and worse and I couldn't contain myself, I yelled for the nurse to bring me the pain medicine, but she said it was too late. 30 minutes to an hour went by, and the nurse and doctor came into my room with this long thing that looked like a crochet hook.

Next thing I knew, it was inserted, and I felt warm water gushing out, "Push, and Push now!"

"I can't it hurts so bad!"

"You need to push so your baby can come out!"

So, I gave a push and then another, and then another, and my baby was out! She was born October 9, 1991 at 4 lbs.; I was only about 7 months pregnant when I had her. She was premature. I didn't get to hold her, and she didn't cry. They cleaned her up and she was gone. I fell asleep for a while, then the doctor comes in and tells me that she's in ICU. Her lungs were not developed, and she was in an incubator. She wouldn't hold down any milk so they wanted me to pump my breast so she could eat.

I never left the hospital and stayed in the Ronald McDonald house. My daughter and I were left alone. She was so very tiny, and I was not allowed to hold her. If I wanted to touch her, I had to wash up and put my hands through these long gloves. I felt bad for her, because she had all these tubes and IV's fighting for her life. She was in ICU for a month and a half. No one came to see her or didn't even check if I needed anything.

She was in ICU, for almost a month longer, but she pulled through and I was finally able to hold her. Her little fingers grabbed onto mine and I felt a love I had never felt before. The doctors and nurses absolutely loved her, but there was no grater love than the one I had for her. She was mine!

I went back to my aunties in Belen, New Mexico, growing a bond with my daughter. It almost felt like I was playing with a Barbie. I got to dress her in all these cute little dresses and take professional pictures with her for Christmas. She was so adorable and little. At night my aunty would come in our room and yell, "Jessica don't you hear the baby?"

I did not hear her crying her pretty little head off. I would get up to feed and or change her and rock her until she fell back asleep. Everything was going fantastic. My baby was healthy, and I was healthy, but needless to say, I went back to partying, leaving my daughter with my aunt. My aunt told me that she can no longer take care of her. She reminded me of a cousin of mine who couldn't have babies.

Long story short, we went through the adoption process when my daughter was 1 years old. I was also told that I can have her back when I got on my feet. That never happened even when I went to visit my daughter, they would tell me she wasn't there, yet I could hear her inside the house. My daughter was kept from me I never got to see her. I've tried to reach out to her as an adult, but she doesn't want anything to do with me. There's nothing more I can do but pray. In God's time!

<u>Life as an Adult</u>

When I turned 18 years old, I was emancipated from an institution in San Marcos, Texas, and was on the streets with an SSI check and nowhere to go. I ended up staying with another aunt, who used to get high and drunk, I fitted right in. This time I was trying acid. I would have to say this was the worst high I've ever experienced, and never did it again.

Along the way I met a guy around my age. We began dating, and immediately I became pregnant. I moved in with him and his family in their trailer that didn't have any working utilities; it made things hard, but at least I had a roof over my head.

From Espanola, New Mexico, we got our own apartment in Albuquerque, New Mexico. A cozy little one bedroom, but it was ours and I loved it! I loved it until he started beating me and kicking me in my stomach while I was 6 months pregnant. He would come and go as he pleased, invited people over to get high, leaving me to fend for myself.

May 21, 1995, I went into labor at 7 ½ months along. I woke up my boyfriend and told him my water broke. I had to get my own things together and walk myself to the car. Once we arrive at the hospital and I got settled in, he says he's going home to shower and leaves me at the hospital by myself. My uncle showed up to support me and hold my hand.

I went into labor and my boyfriend was still not there. So, my uncle went into the delivery room with me. I had a beautiful baby boy 7 lbs. 1 oz. Healthy and no need to keep him in the hospital. I got to take him home the very next day.

Needless to say, my boyfriend never showed up. We were together off and on the next three years with him going in and out of jail. In March of 1998 he got arrested and went to prison. I couldn't afford the rent, so my son and I got evicted. I found a homeless shelter in Santa Fe, where we could stay at.

On August 8, 1998, I heard about an audition for the movie Wild Wild West, with Will Smith and Salma Hayek. I auditioned for Salma's body double. After the audition was over, I was told if they choose me, they will call me in two days. I didn't think anything of it, and I was not expecting for them to call. Late in the evening, two days later, I got the call telling me I was chosen for the part. I couldn't believe what I was hearing. I asked over and over again if this was a prank, and they told me no. I yelled with joy and said, "Thank you so much!"

After I get off the phone, I call the aunt that I lived with when I was pregnant with my daughter and told her the news. I then asked her if she could please do me a favor and watch my son (who is 3 years old at the time) until I was done with the movie. She said yes, and I told her I would be over there in a couple of days.

On my way to Albuquerque, I stop at my female cousins to tell her the news and we ended up drinking. The next day before I took off, her 15-year-old daughter decided she wanted to come with me. We decided to stay at a homeless shelter called Joy Junction.

That night my son and I went to church. As he sat on my lap eating dry cheerios, he said "Mom, I love Jesus and Jesus loves me, huh mom?"

"Yes son"

"And the devil has a knife, huh mom?" "Yes son, now please be quiet so mommy can hear the pastor."

"But mommy one day I'll be with him, huh mom."

"Yes son."

The church service was over, and I needed to find a ride to Mountainair, to get my son to my aunties, because I had to be at my first scene the next morning at 6 am. My cousin sees me and tells me we got a ride. She met this 19-year-old with a car.

On the way out the door, some guy is begging me not to leave, telling me to wait until the morning, because he wanted to cook dinner for me. I kindly declined his offer and called my uncle and his friend because we still needed gas money. My uncle and his friend showed up and give me $17. We head to the gas station to put gas in the car, but the driver said he had money. So, we decide to stop at the liquor store and get something to drink and celebrate my part in the movie.

We go into the liquor store and bought 3 different kinds of malt beer and 5 different kinds of hard liquor. As we were leaving, I ask the young guy if I can drive and he said yes. It was him and my son in the back, and myself and cousin in the front.

On the way my son falls asleep. I pulled over and unbuckle him, because I noticed the seatbelt was cutting into his side. I'm now drinking much more and much faster. I saw a train track up ahead and a windy road. I began to panic and slammed on the brakes and hit the 65-mph sign and we began to roll. The car comes to a stop, with the top of the car on the ground.

I remember yelling and crying, "JJ? Where's JJ?"

My cousin came back to the car and I was trapped. She said she couldn't find him.

"Please find him." I went in and out of consciousness. In the background I heard the helicopters. "Where's my son?" I ask one of the paramedics.

"He's okay, just stay calm." They tried pulling me out but could not because my right shoulder was jammed into the gear shift. They had to use the Jaws of Life to get me out. Once I was out, I was placed on the helicopter with my son and taken to the hospital. I was unaware what happened to my cousin and the young fellow.

Instead of shooting a movie September 1998 I was sentenced to 12 years in the New Mexico's Woman's prison for 2 counts of Vehicular Homicide and great bodily injury. My cousin came out of the accident with a scratch, but the young fellow and my son were pronounced dead. My son died August 18, 1998.

This hit me so hard and I immediately tried to kill myself. During my entire incarceration, I tried to kill myself over 50 times; I lost count. I was placed in a mental hospital my second year in prison. I was released September 15, 2006 to the streets once again.

With nowhere to go, a lot of pain and hatred towards myself, I fell into the drug and alcohol world again, this time much deeper.

I started using heavier drugs and quickly became addicted. I kept going in and out of jail and a couple of times back to University of New Mexico Mental Health adult ward. More suicide attempts and rebel like behavior. I found myself in this vicious cycle I could not get myself out of. I tried therapy, medication, street drugs, and fighting, but I seemed to dig myself a deeper hole that was harder and harder to get out of.

Family and strangers would tell me about God, and I would say, "I know, I know." I've been searching for some type of healing and felt a void that no one or nothing could fill. I knew God was a loving and forgiving God, but because he was not physical, I never gave him a chance.

I was in and out of violent relationships, getting high, drunk, and selling drugs. I once again got caught up and ended up in jail, serving another 6 months in county. I got out on probation and hit the streets again, this time on my way to California. I reached out to my youngest sister and asked her for help. I told her I was in a motel and was addicted to crack really badly, and I wanted out of New Mexico. I told her I really wanted a change, a new way of life.

She agreed to buy my train ticket. I had been talking to a female since 2004 while incarcerated in prison, and we agreed to meet. She also sent me money to eat on the way. I called an uncle of mine, on my mom's side, and asked if he could give me a ride to the train station. He said yes and was there about 30 minutes later. We went to eat, I got him gas for the car and then he dropped me off.

When I got to Victorville, California, I stayed with my mom and brothers for a while, but that was not working for me. I got hooked on meth and was doing bad. I asked my sister if I could please stay with her and she agreed. I was there about 2 months when I was kicked out for dating a female. I called this girlfriend of mine and told her I had nowhere to go, she helped me rent a room in someone's house.

While living there, the woman's daughter kept going in my room and I didn't appreciate that. My privacy was being violated and wanted out of the contract. She said I was not going to get my deposit back. Naturally I got mad, grabbed my things and left. My girlfriend spoke to her father and he agreed to let me stay in the mobile home in their front yard. I had access to the bathroom in the house, but mostly I stayed in the mobile home.

Little by little I moved inside the house. After I was there for a couple of months my girlfriend, her 6-year-old daughter, and I got an apartment. This relationship lasted for about 6 years. After our relationship was over, once again I ended up back on the streets getting high and getting into trouble. In and out of jail, more abusive relationships, and more time lost. I was in a relationship that was so bad I could not find a way out.

One day, my boyfriend went to do something, and I realized this was my chance to leave. I guzzled down a beer got on my bicycle and took off as fast as I could. I stopped at a Starbucks, so I could figure out my next step. As I was sitting there, a white car pulled up with an older couple in it, as the man got out the passenger side he asks, "What's wrong sweetie?"

I told him nothing was wrong, and he proceeded to say, "I know something is wrong."

First, I didn't understand how he knew something was troubling me, because this man is blind. His wife went inside and bought me a coffee while we talked, and I told him about my addiction and abusive relationship. When his wife came out, she told me that they hardly ever drink coffee and they were not going to come to Starbucks that night, but they thought they deserved a treat. Then she said, "Now I know why we came, God sent us to help you!"

She made some calls and got me into a domestic violent shelter in Ridgecrest, California, which was more than 2 hours away. Before we set out, they took me to eat twice and once at Denny's when we got there. When we were done eating, she followed me to the bathroom to talk to me. She said to follow God and keep him close, then she took off her bracelet that her husband gave her for their anniversary and told me to keep it. She put the bracelet on my wrist, hugged me, kissed me on my cheek, and told me she loved me, but most of all God loved me more!

We left Denny's and met a staff member from the shelter outside. They wished me well and to the shelter I went. I was there about 3 weeks when I began looking for a job. I sobered up and in about one month I was working at Walmart and Merry Maids part time. I began doing really well, talking care of my responsibilities, staying sober, minding my P's and Q's. I met this guy on a dating site and we became friends. I moved in with him, his kids, and nanny.

One night I was walking down the street and met this guy and he asked me if I was looking for anything. I knew what he meant and even though I knew I shouldn't have, my mouth said yes. I gave him my money and off he went to get me some meth. I kept getting high while working, eventually I lost my job and I was back to square one.

My friend told me I had to leave by Christmas, because his wife was moving back in and there was not enough room for all of us. I didn't move out until around February and when I did, I had told him I was getting high. He personally didn't associate with people who used, but he said he saw something in me and didn't want to give up on me.

When I did move out, I got a settlement and I promised I wouldn't spend a dime on drugs; oh, was that promise broken. I bought clothes for others, took them out to eat, and even gave them money. Back to another abusive relationship while taking care of this man's two children.

One time he picked me up by my throat and slammed my head through the hall closet door, and then slammed me to the ground. I laid there and pretended to be knocked out. The entire time he was yelling at me, telling me how it was my fault for what he did.

He's punched me in my mouth loosening a tooth that later fell out.

Every time I tried to leave he would sit by the door so I couldn't. He told his friends that I was the one who was crazy; yeah, crazy for not calling the cops when I should have.

One time, I did chase him with scissors, because I was tired of the abuse. From then on, I made sure to carry a knife, scissors, or some type of sharp object in case he lunged at me. After the scissors incident he knew I had carried a weapon and most of the time he left me alone!

A friend of mine, name Brian, came over unexpectedly. When he was about to leave, I told my boyfriend that I wanted to leave. He looked shocked. What could he possibly do now that there was someone here witnessing me not wanting to be there? He said, "You want to leave?"

I said, "Yes."

He said, "Then get the (bleep) out of here!"

Brian was standing in the doorway, I asked him, "Please don't go, please wait for me." He said, "I'll wait here."

As I walk into the bedroom to get my things, that had been secretly packed for the day I was able to disappear, I looked over my shoulder to make sure Brian wasn't going to leave and pleaded with him again, "Please don't leave, please wait for me!

I gathered my things and literally ran out the door. I took my things to Brian's house, and after that, we went dumpster diving. For those of you who don't know what dumpster diving is, it's going through trash cans and dumpsters looking for things or recyclables that people no longer want and throw away.

When we got back to Brian's house, we sat there talked and giggled;

something I hadn't done for years. As time went by, we become closer and we began to date. After my money ran, out we slept on the streets and eventually he got arrested for an old warrant. I stayed with his mom for a couple of months while he was in jail. After jail he was sent to a program for veterans in Los Angeles.

He wanted me closer to him, so his mom took me and all of our belongings and dropped me off, again on the streets with nowhere to go. I slept outside while he was in a program and people would get mad about my situation asking why I am on the streets while he was inside nice and warm.

Of course, I defended him, telling them that he is getting his act together and I'm there to support him. I tried to get into many rehabilitation centers, but could not because I did not have insurance in L.A. County. I remained sober while sleeping outside the gate of Brian's program. After a few months of sleeping outside, I found out about a shelter in Santa Ana. I stayed there for about 4 months, but I got drunk one night and decided not to go back. Once again, I was sleeping outside the gate of Brian's program.

It was getting cold outside and I told Brian I needed a car. I asked if he was willing to sell his motorcycle to get me a car. At first it was hard to convince him to sell it, but eventually he gave in. During the time I was looking for a car, I stayed with his mom. In those 3 weeks I found myself revisiting the boyfriend who use to abuse me. Why?

I don't know, but eventually I started getting high again. I spoke to Brian every day on the phone and told him I was getting high again and he told me to bring him some. I ended up buying a car that was a lemon from my ex which broke down on me on my way to Los Angeles. I brought Brian some drugs and he began using again. The car was towed outside the fence of his program where other homeless people slept.

I began selling drugs, then he got involved in doing the same thing. I started selling to the guys who were in the program with him. We got arrested twice for sales. December 10th, 2018, at 4 o'clock in the morning, I was tired of being sick and tired, and we knew we needed a change. I fell to my knees hysterically, crying asking God to please help. I told him I didn't want to live like this anymore. "PLEASE HELP ME!"

Around 8:00 am, Brian and I began cooking in a small trash can, and around 8:30 am right when our food was done, some cops and undercover cops showed up and told, about 11 of us, to get on our knees. We got searched along with our things, questioned; cold metal was placed on our wrist. Off to jail Brian and I went for the third time.

After a few court hearings, we decided to take our cases to trial, because we were charged with sales of methamphetamines, but no drugs were found on us. We would have won our case, but we decided to go to a program because we had nothing to go to but the street. We would have gone back to what we knew best, the life of drugs, homelessness, and crime.

I went to a program while Brian stayed in jail waiting for his program. A month later he was accepted into U.S. Vets. I stayed at the program for 2 ½ months before I decided to leave. Back to the streets getting high and selling drugs again. We went back to jail and waited for another program. I waited for a program called Project 180 to accept and pick me up. The program was 1 year long, 3 months inpatient and 9 months outpatient. Brian's program was the same, but at a different facility.

I graduated the 90-day program and am in outpatient now. In the meantime, I have held a job, go to meetings, and am currently working on my steps for N.A. with a sponsor. I have had all 100% progress reports, as well as Brian. I am so proud to say that Brian and I have been sober for over a year, as of December 11, 2019! I graduate my program in February 2020 and Brian in April 2020. When we graduate, our charges will be dropped and expunged. No probation and no more contact with the courts!

My attitude has changed tremendously, and my faith in God keeps growing and growing! I thank God every day for never giving up on me, for keeping me safe when I should have been dead. I show God my appreciation by doing His will, doing what he asks of me, being kind to others, staying away from the people who have hurt me, not going back to my old ways, being in His word every day, putting to practice what I tell others, talking to God on a daily basis, telling others about God, and doing as Jesus would do, even though I can and never will come even remotely close to being like him, which is perfect.

God has and will help all of us more than any human can! PERIOD! Remember this saying, "Tell me who you hang around with, and I will tell you who you are!"

Proverbs 3:5-6 says; *5 "Trust in the Lord with all your heart and lean not on your own understanding; 6 in all your ways submit to him, and he will make your paths straight."*

The overall lesson was to speak and stand up for myself. Not to worry what others might think of me. If I didn't care for is going to care for me. No matter the situation, always and I mean always tell the truth. Don't sugar coat or hide anything for anyone. The truth will always come to light. Help those that are in need, because at one time we were in need or will be in need.

If you see something that doesn't meet the eye, PLEASE, say something. Don't just turn your heads. A lot of the human race is afraid to speak. Don't be one of them. Help those that are not able to help themselves.

If you're in a situation now, don't allow it to go on any longer. The longer you wait, the harder it is to get out of it. Abuse, whether it be Physical, Mental, Emotional or Verbal towards humans and or animals, IS NOT OK! If something is not reported by the Seeing Eye, one is just as guilty for the turn of their head. By helping another person out, the feeling you will possess inside will be rewarding. Not only are others watching, but most importantly GOD is watching you at all times!

Integrity is the key. Luke 12:2-3, that the secrets will be uncovered, the truth will come forth, and God's thought about every behavior and action will be vindicated. What's done in the dark will come to light and thank God he has created it to do so!

Even though I had not said anything for a long time, in God's time, the truth did in fact come to the light. Be vigilant and aware of what others might be blind to. Matthew 7:12 *"Therefore whatever you desire for men to do to you, shall also do to them; for this is the law and the prophets."*

The mistakes I made were not reaching out to God earlier in life. That would have saved me a lot of problems and heart aches. Satan was the main distraction in my life. He knew I was chosen by God and wanted to see me fail, and I was blind to this. Not wanting to abide by the law and do my own thing kept me even further away from God.

I learned that God is the truth, the way, and the light; doing our own will and not God's, we will always fail. When we decide to surrender and abide in him, then and only then, will we have peace and comfort. I changed dramatically and with this change, others followed to live a better and healthier life.

The overall lesson is there is no success or peace without our loving father on our side. We all have the same story just different experiences. It's never too late to reach out to God and ask for help.

It's never too late to turn a negative into a positive, but willpower and faith is needed. It starts with being submissive to God! If things continuously seem to go wrong, and you cannot seem to catch a break in life, then look back and see what areas you might need help in.

God sees and hears everything; he is just waiting for you to call upon him. Matthew 7:7 says; *"Ask and it will be given to you; seek and you will find; knock and the door will be opened to you."*

If you do not know how to pray, it's simply having a conversation, as if you are talking to a friend. God is our friend and he will listen. Have an open heart and mind, and things will fall into place. Thank you, Jesus, I give you all the credit, I honor you and I love you!

Once I started putting God first in my life, I began to see results. He does not promise all days will be perfect, because only he is perfect. He does promise a way out. 1 Corinthians 10:13 says, *"No temptation has overtaken you except what is common to mankind. And God is faithful; he will not let you be tempted beyond what you can bear. But when you are tempted, he will also provide a way out so that you can endure it."*

A valuable lesson I learned is, it's better to give than it is to receive. It's ok to let someone go in front of you in a grocery line. If someone has their blinker on and their trying to switch lanes, let them in.

Take time to do the things you love, cherish the moments, forget the past, don't worry about tomorrow, and live in the present like it's your last day on earth! Remember the smallest things might not mean much to you but may mean the world to others!

I opened my story with Jeremiah 29:11, because no matter where I went, I saw this scripture on various things, like a pillow, a book bag, or a journal. I knew God was sending me a message, so I held on to this scripture knowing I was NEVER ALONE!

Lord I come to you and ask for protection for those who know you and those who don't. Put your arms around them and allow them to feel your love, joy, and peace. Allow them to feel your presence so they know they're not alone. Comfort and guide them as they take this journey through life. In Jesus' mighty name I pray...Amen!

Philippians 4:13
"I can do all things through Christ who strengthens me"!

God bless y'all on your journeys!
With a loving heart and God's love,
Your sister in Christ
Jessica D.K. Romero

Jessica D.K. Romero

Jessica is from a small town in New Mexico called Mountainair. She has lived in Los Angeles for the past 12 years. Jessica is currently engaged to a wonderful man. She has stayed focused on the present and does not worry about tomorrow! Her faith in God continues to grow and grow every day! She enjoys helping others in any way she can and hopes to help more along the way.

www.ingramcontent.com/pod-product-compliance
Lightning Source LLC
LaVergne TN
LVHW011336080426
835513LV00006B/372